Can We Save The Planet?

The Big Idea

Alice Bell

Can We Save The Planet?

A primer for the 21st century

Over 190 illustrations

General Editor:
Matthew Taylor

Contents

Introduction

A

What, in the 2020s, does it mean to save the planet? Can we? Should we? Whose planet is it anyway?

When green activists shout 'Save the planet', there is always some know-it-all who is quick to explain: 'The planet does not need saving, actually. The Earth has seen a lot worse than us before, and will be fine long after we are gone. It is people we need to worry about.' This is a tempting critique, a reminder, perhaps, to us humans not to be too egotistical. After all, there is a whole universe out there that is much bigger and stronger than we are.

The reality is that humans have long been an integral part of the Earth. As philosophers of science and technology Bruno Latour (b. 1947) and Donna Haraway (b. 1944) both argue, we humans live interconnected lives, not only with each other but with other animals, plants and machines too. There are differences and inequalities of power between non-humans and us, just as there are differences and inequalities of power between humans, but this does not make us somehow separate from the rest of life on Earth. Humans cannot live their lives detached from all other life on Earth. We have the power to harness its resources and harm its ecosystems. It is time we acknowledged that power and the responsibility that goes with it.

A   Visitors to Glacier Point,
     California, take in the view,
     2019. This 2,199-metre
     (7,215-ft) granite precipice
     reaches over Yosemite Valley,
     offering a view of the parks'
     most famous landmarks.
     The USA's first national park,
     Yosemite has attracted
     tourists since the mid 19th
     century. Today, it attracts
     millions of visitors every year,
     with Glacier Point one of the
     most popular photo spots.
B   The famous 'Vashon Island
     Bike Tree' in Washington, USA.
     Myth has it that a boy tied his
     bike to a tree before going off
     to World War I, never to return.
     It is more likely that the bike
     dates back to the 1950s
     when the tree was a sapling.
     The image of nature seemingly
     capturing technology
     has made the sight
     internationally famous.

B

A

Today, the term 'tree-hugger' tends to be used to dismiss environmentalists: people who are dreamily more interested in plants than in their fellow humans. But the first recorded tree-huggers – a group of Bishnoi villagers in Rajasthan, India – were acutely aware of the importance of trees in nature. In 1730, a number of Khejri trees were due to be felled to build a new palace for Abhai Singh, the Raja of Marwar (now Jodhpur). The local people relied on the trees' shade, leaves, sap and bark. Understandably, the trees had grown to hold cultural significance for the community, too. One villager, Amrita Devi, said she would rather die than see the trees cut down. The axe men took her at her word and chopped her head off in place of a tree. Her three daughters followed their mother's lead, paying the same price, and soon other villagers began to hug the remaining trees tight, putting their bodies clearly in the way of the axes. This action spread to other parts of the region, and more than 360 tree-huggers lost their lives while protecting their trees. When the Raja heard of the bloodbath, he declared the village would never again be compelled to provide wood for the kingdom.

Hurt trees, and often you end up hurting people, too. Save a whale, and you will support humanity's continued survival (if nothing else, their faeces is highly effective at absorbing our carbon emissions).

But we are not talking about the odd tree or whale any more. Between the various ways we humans have found to pollute our air, waters and land – all baked with a portion of anthropogenic climate change – we have gone from one speedily shrinking ice cap to the other, leaving plastic-filled seas, scorched forests, barren reefs, depleted soils and swallowed-up islands in our wake. The latest United Nations (UN) projections put between 500,000 and 1 million species at risk of extinction, many within decades, with humans' impact on the planet the major driver of harm.

This will always come back to bite us. Even the most modern of human lives are ultimately based on nature. Disrupt the ecosystems around us, and we disrupt ourselves. We need healthy forests, clean waterways and rich soils, for food, clean air, clean water, medicine and a sense of well-being.

Anthropogenic climate change is caused by the actions of humans rather than the Earth's natural processes or solar activity.

A   A selection of pictures created on 21 June 2019 showing types of waste found on the Mer de Glace, France's largest glacier, after the melting of ice earlier that month.

B   An Extinction Rebellion activist occupies a tree in Parliament Square, as police attempt to clear the area. It was one of four sites occupied in central London, UK, for a week during April 2019.

C   A tree house in the ancient Hambach Forest, Germany. Tree-sitting is an established trope of environmental activism, and the Hambach treehouses have become a symbol in the fight against deforestation.

We have come to dominate our planet to such an extent that scientists talk about a whole new geological epoch: the Anthropocene. Previous epochs were bookended by meteorite strikes or sustained volcanic eruptions. The Anthropocene was triggered by human activity, and it is continued human activity that has resulted in the environmental crisis that faces us today.

In this new era the old concern that humans should not get too carried away with their power is perhaps misplaced. Maybe it is better to admit the power we hold, before it is too late? Furthermore, our prosperity is too dependent on the rest of the planet to make lazy comments about the Earth being okay without us: we need to save the Earth to save humankind. Whatever your passion, be it economic justice, dismantling the patriarchy or simply having a peaceful picnic in the park with your friends, everything is getting harder, riskier and scarcer because of the damage we have wrought on nature. So, rather than disengage from the Earth we should stop harming it and start restoring it.

A

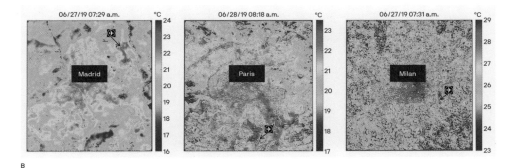

06/27/19 07:29 a.m.　°C

24
23
22
21
20
19
18
17
16

Madrid

06/28/19 08:18 a.m.　°C

23
22
21
20
19
18
17

Paris

06/27/19 07:31 a.m.　°C

29
28
27
26
25
24
23

Milan

B

The **Anthropocene** is the current geological epoch, characterized by the impact of humans on the planet and on the rest of life on Earth.

Global warming refers to an increase in the global average temperature, and is measured in degrees Celcius (or Fahrenheit) above the global average temperature in 1850 (the date that is agreed as 'above pre-industrial levels').

And yet, most of the time, we act as if nothing much is happening. We have got used to talking about stopping climate change as though it is a threat we have to worry about in the future. This attitude might be fine if we were living in the 1950s. However, we have already caused around 1°C (1.8°F) of global warming and people are already suffering from the impact, seen in more severe and more frequent droughts, hurricanes, floods and heatwaves as well as higher food prices. Indeed, we were already a third of the way to 1°C (1.8°F) in the 1930s, and records show that the Arctic started warming as early as the 1830s.

A　The InterContinental Shanghai Wonderland. Built inside a disused quarry pit, this luxury hotel has been described as a 'groundscraper' as 16 of its 18 storeys are below ground, and famously feature several underwater rooms.

B　Heatmaps of the 2019 European heatwave, taken by NASA from the International Space Station. Airports are highlighted as they have a high concentration of heat-retaining surfaces (e.g. concrete).

Words such as 'we' and 'us' get used frequently in 21st-century discussions of the environment, not least because they put the emphasis on the role of humans: we did this; it is up to us to change it. But some of us are more insulated from the impacts of environmental damage than others, and some of us are causing more harm than others. Humans are, currently, a very unequal bunch. As Oxfam points out, the richest 10% of the world's population is responsible for almost half of total lifestyle consumption emissions. By contrast, the poorest 50% contribute only 10%.

INTRODUCTION

13

A

The good news is that we can still change our industries and behaviours to avoid too much further warming, just as we can replant forests we have felled, restore soils and clean up waters we have polluted (indeed, doing these things will also help us tackle climate change). What we do in the next decade is vital. Currently, the window of opportunity is still open, but it is closing rapidly. The time to act is now. It would have been better if we had acted yesterday, but today will do and tomorrow will not.

The following chapters explain how we got into this mess, describe the situation as it currently stands and outline some of the ways we can prevent it from becoming too dystopic. They also invite you to think about which of the various options we want to take. Because we do have options, and each one has its own pros and cons.

The time has come to stop debating whether we should prevent environmental catastrophe, and instead start deciding how to go about it.

1. The Human Planet

A

The **atmosphere** is the layers of gases that surround the Earth, and that are kept in place by the planet's gravity.

The **Anthropocene Working Group** is tasked by the International Commission on Stratigraphy to explore whether and how scientists might officially add the Anthropocene to the geologic time scale. Its membership includes an international mix of earth scientists and archaeologists, as well as experts from history, law and journalism, but has been criticized for being too male and rich-world dominated (parodied online as the 'manthropocene').

We do not just live on this planet; we have shaped it. Each year, the work of humans moves more soil, rock and sediment than is transported by all other natural processes combined. If you took all humans and their domesticated animals (pets and livestock), their combined mass would be greater than all wild terrestrial vertebrates taken together. Humans have left their mark in the chemistry of the air around them, the rocks, the oceans and the **atmosphere**. For the first time in Earth's 4.5-billion-year history, a single species is dictating its future.

Welcome to the Anthropocene.

B

A   Mountain Pass Rare Earth Mine, California, USA. In the 1960s it provided europium for colour television sets. Today it supplies neodymium, key to many so-called 'green' techs, such as wind turbines and electric cars.

B   Aerial view of herdsmen and their cows waiting for buyers at Kara cattle market in Lagos, Nigeria. One of the largest markets in West Africa, thousands of cows pass through it each week.

What is the start date for this epoch? This is a hotly contested question within earth sciences, one that allows us to dig back through the ways in which we built our human planet. The most recent option is 1945, or, more specifically, 5:29 a.m., 16 July 1945, when the first detonation of a nuclear weapon – code name Trinity – was conducted by the US Army in the desert of New Mexico.

This is the timestamp favoured by the Anthropocene Working Group. It is far more than political symbolism. For earth scientists to recognize this as a geologically significant moment, they need to be able to see a record of it in the planet itself. It cannot be merely written in the history books; it has to be transcribed into the Earth.

This is one of the reasons why the Trinity test is so attractive: we can trace markers of its blast of radiation.

A

To explore markers like these and help us put them in context, a specialism of earth sciences, paleoclimatology, uses information left in the Earth itself to build a picture of past environments. Rings in trees, for example, reflect the environment within which each layer grew, acting as natural time capsules. Corals have similar rings. Scientists can also look at the chemical make-up of shells left in sediments on the beds of lakes and oceans.

Polar researchers take cores of ice, drawn from deep inside ancient glaciers. Each slice of these cores is made up of snow that fell in a different year, and exploring their chemistry can offer crucial clues to what the Earth was like back then. Bubbles of air trapped inside the ice provide samples of past atmospheres, and from these scientists can measure the concentration of gases, including carbon dioxide. Beyond EPICA, a huge $12-million European project, is currently researching an area of East Antarctica for ice that is more than 1.5 million years old.

From caves in northern Italy to lakes in China, tree rings in the Amazon, ice buried in the Arctic, or Bermudan corals, scientists can trace finger-prints of cold war nuclear testing, peaking with the Nuclear Test Ban Treaty in 1963. One of these markers, the radioactive isotope of carbon, Carbon-14, has a half-life of about 5,750 years. This means it will be around for scientists to find for tens of thousands of years.

The 1945 date is attractive because of the swift rise in the human population after World War II. Planetary scientists are increasingly describing the past 70 or so years as the Great Acceleration, a period marked by a major expansion in human population. The world's human population has been growing continuously since famine and plague in mid-14th-century Europe. It reached 1 billion for the first time around 1804. It was another 123 years before it grew to 2 billion in 1927, but it took only 33 years to reach 3 billion in 1960. Thereafter, the global population increased to 4 billion in 1974, 5 billion in 1987, 6 billion in 1999 and 7 billion in somewhere between October 2011 and March 2012 (depending on which data you use). Much of this can be seen as positive: we have more people because we are not dying of hunger and disease. But more people can cause more environmental damage.

Paleoclimatology is the study of past climates using imprints found in organisms, ice cores, tree rings and sediment cores.

A   Cross sections of a silver fir trunk (left) and a black locust tree trunk (right). The study of tree rings can give scientists vital clues about the historical environments that these trees grew in.
B   Chinese scientist He Jianfeng collecting an ice-core sample at the North Pole. Examining ice cores is key to our modern scientific understanding of how the climate has changed over time.
C   Geoff Hargreaves, curator at the US National Ice Core Laboratory, surrounded by ice cores. Based in Denver, Colorado, the laboratory stores ice cores from multiple expeditions as a repository for current and future investigations.

B

C

Over the past few hundred years, we have increasingly arranged ourselves around technologies that have allowed us to live longer and often happier lives, but we have left a larger ecological footprint as a result. Plastic is a good example, perhaps the exemplar invention of the Anthropocene: a human attempt at making our own material rather than exploiting nature; first as a replacement for ivory in billiard balls and then instead of shellac, a resin secreted by the female lac bug and used as an insulating material in the electricity industry. Plastic is extremely useful and also immensely polluting. It was first developed in the late 19th century, given a boost during military applications in the 1940s and diffused via domestic consumer markets from the 1950s. Plastic has since piled up to become a major problem.

A

A Women working at the Columbus Plastic Company, Ohio, 1948. The plastic industry was given a boost by military research during World War II and boomed afterwards as domestic markets opened up.
B Springwell Colliery Engine No. 2, built by Robert Stephenson in 1826. It was used to move wagons of coal, in this case for a mine in the north east of England.
C James Watt's workshop. This is one of a series of photographs taken when the workshop was being moved to the Science Museum, London, UK, in December 1924, where you can still see it on display.

B   C

Plastic is only part of the puzzle though, and many scientists want to look much further back than the 20th century for the start of the Anthropocene. After all, we have been industrializing in various forms for thousands of years, polluting the planet along the way. The ghosts of Roman copper smelting can be found in Greenland ice cores, for example. During the Industrial Revolution of the late 18th century, things really heated up, literally, as the start of our addiction to fossil fuels fed more carbon dioxide into the atmosphere, fuelling global warming. And if we want a marker left in the Earth's record to compete with the Trinity test as a start date for the Anthropocene, the 1830s must be a contender because the Arctic has been warming since that time.

Fossil fuels such as coal and oil have been used by humans in different parts of the world, and in various ways, for thousands of years. However, it was not until the 18th century that we burnt them on industrial levels. The first key invention was the steam engine by Thomas Newcomen (1664–1729) in 1712, which provided a way to pump water out of mines speedily. Several decades later, James Watt (1736–1819) patented steam engines suitable for driving factory machinery, and the technology spread, increasing the market for coal in the process. By the end of the 18th century, people were illuminating buildings using gas made from burning coal. By the mid-19th century, commercial coal gas works were supplying light and heat to homes and businesses in cities around the world.

Renewable energy comes from sources that will be replenished within human timescales. Examples include energy from sunlight (either to produce electricity or heat), wind, rain, tides, waves and geothermal heat. It can also refer to biofuels, energy produced from plants.

Sperm oil is not technically an oil, more a wax. It burns brightly and does not smell as much as other forms of whale oil, which are produced from boiling the blubber.

A

Richard Trevithick (1771–1833) developed high-pressured engines that were small enough to be used on trains around the beginning of the 19th century, and by the start of the 20th, these had been joined by engines that ran on petrol/gasoline or diesel produced from oil.

The age of cars and aeroplanes had begun.

The world's first coal-fired electricity station – the Edison Electric Light Station – opened in London, UK, in January 1882. By the following September, it had a cousin in New York, USA. As we found new and exciting ways to use electricity, whole new reasons to burn extensive quantities of fossil fuels opened up. The seeds for a renewable energy future were also planted, with the first homes lit by hydropower and wind turbines in the 1880s.

Throughout this period, we were also hunting and killing whales for fuel, thereby driving some species to extinction. Whale oil was used to light houses and streets, and as the Industrial Revolution shifted working culture, it came to be utilized to light factories so employees could work longer hours. In the middle of the 19th century, when Herman Melville (1819–91) was penning *Moby Dick* (1851), whaling was a booming global industry, the fifth largest sector in the US economy. Of the more than 700 whaling ships on the world's oceans in the 1840s, more than half were based out of the Massachusetts port of New Bedford, USA, known as 'the city that lit the world'. Whalers would haul the giant beasts onto their ships, cut off their heads and bail out thousands of litres of sperm oil. It has been estimated that, by 1880, the sperm whale population had declined by nearly a third due to whaling. But fossil fuels gradually edged out whale oil, and by the mid-20th century, following scientific advice on whale populations, many countries had banned whaling altogether. The rise and fall of the whaling industry makes for an interesting case study as an example of humans changing their behaviour before it was entirely too late. Once upon a time, we mined whales for oil; now we do not. Perhaps one day soon we will look back on the days we mined coal and find that practice equally unacceptable.

The Industrial Revolution was not only about energy.

A   Engravings taken from *The Natural History of the Ordinary Cetacea or Whales* by William Jardine (1837). The first shows fishermen harpooning a Greenland whale that has tossed one of the attacking boats and the second shows fishermen harpooning a sperm whale. By 1880, the sperm whale population had declined by nearly a third due to whaling.
B   Greenwich generating station, London, UK, 1906. Built in 1902 by London County Council to provide electricity for trams, it was originally coal-fired. It is still used as a back up for London's underground rail system.

There was a host of other inventions, which not only opened up new markets and ways to live, but also found alternative ways to eat up and pollute the natural world in the process. In 1798 in France, Louis-Nicolas Robert (1761–1828) patented a machine for making a continuous sheet of paper on a loop of wire fabric, later to become the scourge of forests the world over. The greater availability of paper and cloth also paved the way for disposable products. The uptake of disposability was driven in part by the emerging advertising industry and consumer culture, but also by concerns over hygiene. Today, our love of disposable products remains extremely damaging, especially since it has been combined with the invention of plastics, thus creating new risks in ocean pollution just as it avoids more immediate health ones.

In 1824, a Leeds bricklayer, Joseph Aspdin (1778–1855) patented a chemical process for combining clay and limestone at high temperatures to produce Portland cement. Today, the cement industry has grown to be one of the world's primary carbon dioxide polluters, producing about 8% of global emissions.

A   Advertisements from the 1890s, showing the rise of consumer culture. The products on display in these adverts also show how disposable packaging provided a handy canvas for the emerging advertising industry.
B   More advertisements from the same era from the USA, France and Russia. By the start of the 20th century, advertising had become an international industry.

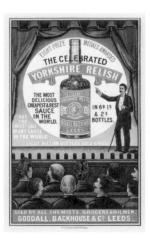

A

So far, we have looked at two contenders for the start of the Anthropocene.

First, the growth of the post-war era marked by proxy through the radioactive fallout of the 1945 Trinity test. And second, the industrial developments of the 18th and 19th centuries, viewable in signs of warming waters in the 1830s. Some scientists would like to look back a lot further, and consider the way the human practice of farming made its mark on our planet. As we will discuss more in Chapter 2, clearing land for farming contributes to both global warming and biodiversity loss. Cut down a forest, and it no longer absorbs carbon. Whole species can lose their homes, too.

The **Neolithic Revolution** is also known as the first agricultural revolution. Many human cultures moved from a lifestyle of hunting and gathering to one of agriculture and settlement.

Agronomy is the science and technology of producing and using plants for either food or materials.

Farming emerged during the Neolithic Revolution around 12,000 years ago, with another agricultural revolution taking place in the Islamic Golden Age, some 1,200 to 800 years ago. The Romans had done a good job of developing agricultural techniques and spreading various crops around their empire, but the Arabs studied the topic scientifically, intensifying the results. Major works on agronomy were published, disseminating useful techniques on how to grow, for example, olives trees, wheat and barley, and encouraging people to find and experiment with new kinds of crops. Irrigation techniques, such as the sakia water wheel, and several types of fruit and vegetable were spread across the Islamic world.

Europe in the 18th to mid-19th centuries saw another flurry of agricultural development. The refinement of the seed drill by Jethro Tull (1674–1741) in 1701 built on technology that had originated in China and made its way to Europe via India in the middle of the 16th century. There were also improvements to crop rotation, new ploughs and new fertilizers, including the transportation of sodium nitrate deposits from Peru to Britain.

A

A   Guano (seabird and bat excrement) is an effective fertilizer. In the 19th century trade of guano fuelled war and the expansion of colonialist power. It was superseded by artificial fertilizers after World War II.

B   Humans have been changing the shape of plants and animals around them long before genetic modification became an option, as these 19th-century depictions of prize winningly large animals show.

B

People had been experimenting with the selective breeding of wheat, rice, horses and dogs for millennia, but it was around the middle of the 18th century that great advances were made, and a century later that, via Charles Darwin (1809–82), people started talking about the science behind it. Sheep were bred for wool or meat; cows were bred not only to pull a plough but also for their meat.

A 2018 study published by the Royal Society argues that the chicken offers an especially good example of how our approach to feeding ourselves has dominated the planet. Chicken meat consumption is growing faster than any other meat type; it could soon outpace pork. Since the Chicken-of-Tomorrow programme in the early 1950s, launched to encourage the development of higher meat-yielding birds, chicken farming has developed into a complex mechanized system integrating computer software, transportation vehicles, refrigeration, heating, feed processing factories and more. There are now 23 billion so-called 'broiler' chickens in the world, bred and reared for their ability to feed us. Compare chicken bones from archaeological sites of Roman Britain with those of a modern broiler, and some are triple the width and double the length. Broiler chickens have a life span of five to seven weeks (compared with 11 years for their wild ancestors, and a year for egg-laying hens) and we slaughter 66 billion a year.

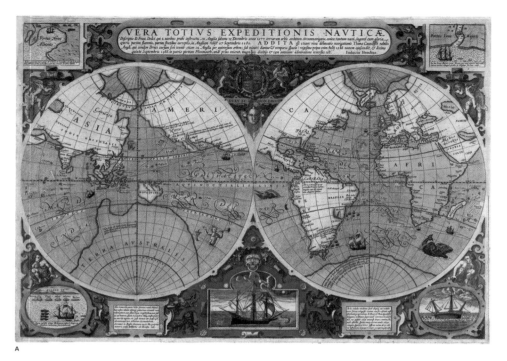

A

Another possible start date to the Anthropocene is 1610, proposed by earth systems scientists Mark Maslin and Simon Lewis. With this, they point towards the impact of global trade.

Why 1610? There is an observable dip in atmospheric carbon dioxide. As Maslin and Lewis explain, 50 million indigenous Americans died during the first few decades of the 16th century, following the landing of the Europeans in 1492. The land, previously farmed by these now decimated communities, started to shift back into forests. The trees had, at least temporarily, space to grow without humans cutting them down. This regrowth absorbed enough carbon dioxide to create an observable dip in ice core records around 1610. Some researchers even think it could have contributed to the so-called Little Ice Age.

The **Little Ice Age** was a period from around 1300 to 1850 that seems to have been particularly cold in many parts of the world, with especially cold intervals in 1650, 1770 and 1850. Not cold enough to be a true Ice Age, it was given the title in 1939. Various causes have been suggested, including heightened volcanic activity and decreases in the human population.

The **Orbis Hypothesis** is named from the Latin word for world – 'orbis' – because it focuses on the environmental impact of globalized trade and colonialism following 1492.

The colonization of the Americas also led to a growth of global trade networks that linked Europe to the Americas, and intensified travel to Asia and Africa. For this reason, Maslin and Lewis call their theory supporting the 1610 date as the start of the Anthropocene the Orbis Hypothesis, meaning 'world hypothesis', arguing that it marks the beginning of a modern whole-world system. These new trade routes not only shifted people, but other species, too. Plants were moved by humans from one continent to another: sugar cane, oranges, rice and, eventually, coffee were shipped to the Americas, and potatoes, tobacco, maize and tomatoes from the Americas to Europe. Animals moved, too: horses, cows, pigs and, more by accident than design, several types of earthworm. Chickens were brought to the New World by Spanish colonists in the 16th century. As with much of the Anthropocene, not all of this was necessarily harmful for the environment, even if it was very clearly bad for the many people who were exploited by the system. Some was just new.

The London plane tree offers an iconic example, a now widespread species that would not exist if it were not for this new movement of people around the globe. It is a hybrid of two trees: the American sycamore and the Oriental plane. It is not certain exactly where and when the hybridization took place, possibly in Spain, or in London itself, where the tree was first discovered in the mid-17th century by botanist John Tradescant the Younger (1608–62) in his Vauxhall gardens. The trees were planted in London parks in the 18th century and then in the 19th century, taking inspiration from a Parisian trend for leafy boulevards, they began to line London's streets. In the 20th century, the species was planted throughout Central Park in New York City and even referenced in the park's logo. Hay fever sufferers may curse the London plane, but it is most interesting for simply existing: a combination of two plants that started life on entirely different sides of the world, brought together by the way humans circumnavigated their planet.

A

Many of the botanical stories of colonialism are less benign. Crops such as rice, cotton, breadfruit, tobacco and sugar not only crossed oceans, they also relied on slave labour and, especially when it came to rice, the expertise of enslaved Africans. In the process, slaves bankrolled large parts of the Industrial Revolution, as white people who grew rich off the profits could plough their money into new technologies and research. This is another reason why the Orbis Hypothesis is a good candidate for the start of the Anthropocene: the technologies of the Industrial Revolution share a common, colonialist ancestor with that dip in carbon dioxide in 1610.

Perhaps most interesting, from the perspective of our modern environmental crisis, is the case of the palm oil tree. Native to west and south west Africa, the trees were taken to the Indonesian island of Java by the Dutch in 1848, and then to Malaysia by the British in 1910. Today, Indonesia produces about half of the world's palm oil, with Malaysia providing another third and the rest coming from countries across the tropics, including Thailand, Colombia and Nigeria. You have almost certainly eaten palm oil: in bread, chocolate, ice cream or biscuits. You might have used it in cosmetics or fuel, too.

Between 1980 and 2014, annual global palm oil production increased from 4.5 million tonnes to 70 million tonnes (4.9 million to 77 million tons), and palm oil demand is expected to grow at 1.7% per year until 2050. Industrial-scale oil palm plantations now occupy an area of 18.7 million hectares (46.2 million ac) worldwide (and that figure does not include smallholder plantations). The UN highlights 193 critically endangered, endangered and vulnerable species threatened by palm oil production, including chimpanzees in Nigeria, tigers in Thailand and Indonesia, orangutans in Malaysia and cassowaries in Papua New Guinea.

Whatever date is chosen to start the Anthropocene, there is a profound philosophical point contained in the Anthropocene thesis. As Maslin and Lewis note, it has become commonplace to talk about the history of science as shifting humanity's view of itself further away from the centre of the universe, challenging our egotism. In 1543, Copernicus (1473–1543) published his astronomical model, putting the sun, not Earth, at the centre of the solar system. In 1859, Darwin established humans as simply part of a tree of life with no special origin. Anthropocene thinking turns this on its head, reasserting humans as active agents in Earth's functioning. It should also invite us to consider the inequalities between humans.

B

A   Illustrations from French pharmacist Pierre Pomet's 1737 book, *A compleat history of drugs*, showing, clockwise from top left, harvests of indigo (fabric dye), sugar, roucou (food colouring) and tobacco.

B   Palm oil awaiting shipment in Nigeria, 1922. Until 1934, Nigeria was the world's largest palm oil producer. Palm oil requires much less land than other vegetable oil crops, but the industry is often criticized for driving deforestation.

A

Whether you are disgusted or delighted by this image of a human-dominated planet is often down to personal philosophy or faith. Some developments have undoubtedly been for the good; others are harder to defend. Many sit in between: a mix of inspiring and enraging.

One way to get a grip on the Anthropocene can be found in 18th-century philosophies of the sublime. To philosophers such as Edmund Burke (1729–97), there was a strong distinction between the merely beautiful and the sublime, the latter being somehow terrifying.

For Immanuel Kant (1724–1804), to experience the sublime is more specifically to feel in awe. We can feel small, weak, insignificant or reverential in comparison, although crucially we also recover some sense of superior self-worth with the realization that the mind was able to conceive something so large and powerful in the first place. Such ideas influenced many European and American artists, but they also speak to broader relationships between humans and the rest of the natural world, in particular a changing understanding of who holds the power.

A/B Cathedral Rocks (left) and Vernal Fall (right), both in Yosemite and captured by photographer Carleton Watkins. They reflect the way an aesthetic for the national sublime has continued to be re-packaged for tourism and national identity in the USA. Yosemite was one of Watkins' favourite subjects, and his photographs of the valley are thought to have significantly influenced the United States Congress' decision to preserve it as a National Park.

The classic study *Mountain Gloom and Mountain Glory* (1959) by Marjorie Hope Nicolson (1894–1981) describes how 17th- and 18th-century European explorers transferred a sense of awe once held for God onto the new and vast mountain ranges, waterfalls and rainforests they encountered. Her analysis helps unpick some of the hopes, fears and aesthetics embedded in our historical relationships with natural and built environments. It helps explain why so much science writing is still infused with religious language. Indeed, the texts these explorers inspired and produced were among early forms of popular science.

A

Humanism is a philosophical and ethical stance built around the value, understanding and agency of human beings over supernatural forces.

In his book *American Technological Sublime* (1994) historian of technology David E. Nye (b. 1946) develops this idea further. By Nye's reading, this sense of awe has been transferred once again, this time to modern engineering projects such as bridges, electric lighting or skyscrapers. Because this sublime object is human-made, Nye posits, there is another layer of power involved. We look at it and think, 'Wow, it is huge and we are tiny,' as we might in front of a mountain, but we know that people made these things, not nature or God, so we can feel greater connection to them and, possibly, a greater control over the world, too.

Those of a humanist persuasion might find celebration in this. Still, the idea that we have a connection to something purely because it is human-made ignores the social inequalities wrapped up in any technology. Some of us can build skyscrapers; some of us have to live in their shade. Arguably, this is often part of the reason they are built: they are the castles of their day, designed to show power.

The people who caused the environmental problems are not, most of the time, those who are worst affected by them. There is much that humans share in the Anthropocene – materials, histories, biologies, technologies, powers and dangers – but plenty that we do not share. As Chapter 2 illustrates, we have produced an alarming set of environmental crises.

As things hot up, it will be increasingly difficult for anyone to escape entirely, but the crises will hit some people faster and far harder than others.

B

2. A Crisis Situation

A

In May 2019, the UN released a new report on biodiversity and <mark>ecosystem services</mark>. The results were stark: 1 million species at risk of extinction. Nowadays, more food, energy and materials are being supplied to people around the world than ever before, but we are pushing nature too far. We are undermining nature's ability to continue to provide ecosystem services, and we are irreplaceably threatening its many other contributions, too, from water and air quality to a sense of place, culture, identity and well-being. Bob Watson (b. 1948), the scientist leading the UN project put it bluntly: 'We are eroding the very foundations of economies, livelihoods, food security, health and quality of life worldwide.'

B

Ecosystem services is a term used to describe the various benefits humans obtain for free from the natural environment: clean drinking water and the pollination of crops, for example.

Environmentalists are sometimes mocked for shouting about current and impending crises, but this really is one. In fact, it is several. It is the seas, the air and the soil, with global warming cooking it all, threatening not only the safety of humans, but also that of hundreds of thousands of other species.

A   A piece of the Southern Patagonian Ice Field breaks off and crashes into Lake Argentino, April 2019. This ice field is melting at some of the highest rates on the planet as a result of global warming.

B   A forest fire in the municipality of Tatumbla, Honduras, March 2019. Although human activities tend to spark such fires, rising temperatures leave forests drier, meaning they are more likely to burn.

This chapter outlines the various environmental catastrophes, which, although not always obvious to the naked eye, are unfolding all around us.

To start at the top, physically speaking at least, our atmosphere is being invaded by carbon. We know this because we have been tracking atmospheric carbon dioxide since it first became clear it was a problem, in the late 1950s. A research project was set up in Hawaii by geophysicist Charles David Keeling (1928–2005) and an almost continuous record of the accumulation of carbon dioxide has been kept ever since. The work is now led by his son, Ralph (b. 1959), and the data it provides are known as the Keeling Curve.

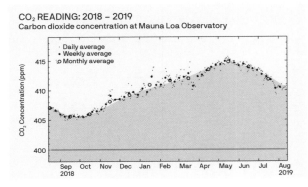

CO$_2$ READING: 2018 – 2019
Carbon dioxide concentration at Mauna Loa Observatory

· Daily average
• Weekly average
○ Monthly average

CO$_2$ Concentration (ppm)

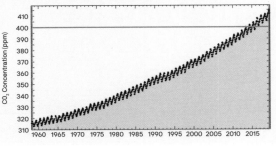

CO$_2$ READING: 1958 – 2019
Carbon dioxide concentration at Mauna Loa Observatory

CO$_2$ Concentration (ppm)

Greenhouse gases are all gases that contribute to the greenhouse effect, the process that occurs when gases in the Earth's atmosphere trap the sun's heat.

Carbon dioxide equivalent describes the global-warming potential of a greenhouse gas, as compared to carbon dioxide. It means that even though each bit of methane, for example, warms more than each bit of carbon dioxide, the gases can be discussed together.

A 'Keeling curve' data on atmospheric carbon dioxide for 2018/2019 (above), and the full record since 1958 (below). The full record presents a zig-zag pattern, resulting from plants in the northern hemisphere releasing CO_2 every autumn as they die and decay.

B A cattle carcass in a ranch on the border between Paraguay and Argentina. The photo is from summer 2016, when the region experienced its worst drought in almost two decades.

Back in March 1958, records show 315 parts of carbon dioxide for every million parts of atmosphere (ppm, or parts per million) and the figure has been rising ever since. In May 2019, it passed the 415-ppm mark for the first time. A little over 400 parts per 1 million might not sound like much, but it is enough to tamper with the basic planetary chemistry our lives rely upon.

Carbon is especially good at trapping heat from the sun. As it blankets the Earth, it keeps us just that little bit warmer. It is a member of a group of so-called 'greenhouse gases'. We need these gases, otherwise it would be unbearably cold, but the atmosphere is too full of them, so the Earth is becoming too hot. Methane and nitrous oxide are also key players, but they only cause about 20% of the problem, and the contribution of other gases such as hydrofluorocarbons and perfluorocarbons is even smaller, less than 5% of the total. The term 'carbon dioxide equivalent' is used as a way to discuss greenhouse gases together.

1°C (1.8°F) of global warming refers to the rise in the Earth's temperature since pre-industrial levels (c. 1850), which was reached in 2015. The Earth's temperature is set to reach 1.5°C (2.7°F) by 2030–50.

A

From paleoclimatology studies, we know that temperatures and carbon dioxide levels have varied over time, but such studies also reveal how extreme recent changes have been. For example, the last time carbon dioxide levels were as high as they are currently, conifer trees grew at the South Pole. More pertinently, sea levels were 20 metres (65 ft) higher, and average global temperatures were 3°C or 4°C (5.4°F or 7.2°F) warmer. This occurred during the Pliocene epoch, between 5.3 million and 2.6 million years ago.

A few degrees Celsius might seem a small amount, but when we are talking about average global temperatures, every fraction of a degree matters. The difference between a 2°C and 1.5°C (3.6°F and 2.7°F) increase, for example, is the difference between having no coral reefs and having about 70% of them.

The harsh reality of climate change is that we already have no choice but to mitigate losses from here on.

Official temperature records have been teetering around 1°C (1.8°F) of global warming for the last few years, and we have been feeling the impact of a gradually warmer world for a lot longer. This is one of the reasons it is so problematic when politicians and campaigners talk about 'catastrophic climate change' as a point we might hit in the future. It is already catastrophic for some people.

B

SIGNAL-TO-NOISE RATIO FROM 1.5°C TO 2°C OF GLOBAL WARMING

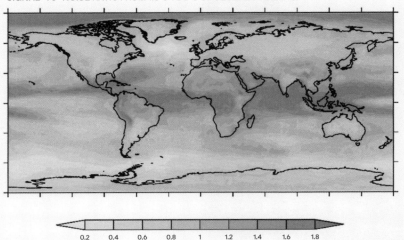

0.2   0.4   0.6   0.8   1   1.2   1.4   1.6   1.8

A major impact of climate change is that seas get bigger as they warm. Rising sea levels swallow land; they also contaminate fresh water sources and leave the land salty. This is already forcing people to relocate. The Marshall Islands – a chain of low-lying volcanic islands and coral atolls in the central Pacific Ocean – lost a fifth of its population to migration between 1999 and 2011, with climate change a clear driver. The Maldives – 1,200 islands across a submarine mountain range 805 kilometres (500 mi) from the tip of India – hit headlines in 2008 when the former president, Mohamed Nasheed (b. 1967), set up a fund to buy new homeland elsewhere. One of his successors then tried to build a new island by pumping sand onto shallow reefs. It is not only islands that are at risk. Bangladesh could lose more than 10% of its land to rising seas in the next few decades, displacing 18 million people. Researchers exploring property prices in Miami point out that those who can afford to choose buy on higher ground, leaving poorer residents to navigate flood risk as best they can.

Coral bleaching refers to the whitening of coral as they expel the algae that give them their characteristic colours. Bleached corals are not dead, but they are at a higher risk of mortality.

A People from Bedono village, Indonesia, use a bridge to escape flooding, June 2017. Formed of more than 17,000 islands, Indonesia is at particular risk of rising sea levels, with many small islands only 1 metre (3.2 ft) above sea level.
B The ruins of a hotel in Abidjan, the economic capital of Ivory Coast. The photo is from summer 2018 after the hotel was destroyed by rising sea levels.
C Flooded homes near Lake Houston, Texas, USA, in the wake of Hurricane Harvey in August 2017. It is estimated that Hurricane Harvey resulted in total costs of $125 billion, second only to Hurricane Katrina ($161 billion).

c

Inside the seas themselves, coral bleaching is one of the most visually dramatic effects of warming waters, even at a global increase of 1°C (1.8°F). As their environment heats up, corals expel the algae (known as zooxanthellae) that live in their tissues and give them their colour, along with the ability to gain energy via photosynthesis. If ocean temperatures rise by just a degree or two over a few weeks, corals turn white, leaving a ghostly skeleton behind. If conditions remain for long enough, the coral dies. Mass coral reef bleaching events have become five times more common over the past 40 years, with the proportion of coral being hit by bleaching each year rising from 8% in the 1980s to 31% in 2016. Despite covering less than 0.1% of the ocean floor, reefs host more than a quarter of all marine fish species, in addition to many other marine animals. The reefs also provide food, protection from flooding and money via tourism, directly supporting more than 500 million people worldwide, including communities such as those in the Maldives who also have to contend with rising sea levels.

Even a small rise in average global temperatures increases the chances and severity of extreme weather events such as heatwaves, heavy rainfall, drought and hurricanes.

A

Such weather phenomena occur anyway, which makes blaming climate change problematic, but each fraction of a degree Celsius global warming makes them worse, and more likely.

Scientists often talk about climate change weighting the dice towards dangerous weather. Again, even at 1°C (1.8°F) global warming, we see various impacts. A study in 2018 of some of the most destructive recent hurricanes – including Katrina (2005), Irma (2017) and Maria (2017) – concludes they were significantly boosted by climate change, as warmer seas ratcheted up rainfall by 5 to 10%. Even Britain, which is relatively insulated from the worst impacts of climate change, suffered a peak in summer deaths in 2018 during an especially hot summer. The Met Office later confirmed that this heatwave had been made about 30 times more likely due to global warming.

Prolonged periods of hot, dry weather can be especially dangerous, as crops fail and land becomes more prone to wildfires and flooding. One of the reasons the floods in Zimbabwe in 2017 were so bad, for example, was because heavy rainfall followed devastating drought. Some cities in the USA are experimenting with drone-based LED displays to replace 4th of July fireworks; the risk of a spark spreading is just too high.

The crisis is deepening. As NASA climate scientist Kate Marvel notes: 'Climate change is not a pass or fail issue' that is game over when we hit a particular point. It would have been easier to tackle climate change if we had started more radical action in the 1980s and 1990s, but we did not, so now will have to do, and it will be far easier than ignoring the issue until the 2040s.

A   As temperatures peak in New York City, USA, people cool off in fountains. Joyful images like these are frequently used to portray heat waves, masking the spike in summer deaths that often accompany them.

B   A woman enjoys a cooling water spray on the banks of the River Seine, Paris, on 25 July 2019. A temperature of 42.6°C (108.7°F) was recorded that day in Paris, France, the highest ever recorded there.

C   Cool water at a cooling centre in a Salvation Army homeless shelter in Northern California, USA. Access to cooling for vulnerable and precariously housed people will become an increasing challenge for cities in the future.

Until the end of 2015, many international climate discussions focused on keeping global warming to less than 2°C (3.6°F). There were even protest signs calling for policies to keep to 2°C (3.6°F), as if this were somehow a safe limit. But 2°C (3.6°F) was never 'safe'; it was more a line some scientists warned we really should not cross because the risk of tipping points increases. Yet politicians grabbed onto this figure as the first stage of negotiating a deadline, as if we had agreed that 2°C (3.6°F) was not ideal but we could probably work around it.

The 2015 Paris climate talks finally acknowledged this issue, arguably way too late, and upped ambition, looking again at the possibility of keeping global warming to 1.5°C (2.7°F). As a result the UN commissioned the Intergovernmental Panel on Climate Change (IPCC) to report on the feasibility of this aim, which was published to some global outcry in October 2018. The message was clear. It is possible to achieve this target, but it will require radical social change like nothing we have seen before. Occasionally, a well-meaning think tank points towards other forms of rapid transitions: ATM machines, the shift from coal gas to natural gas, the uptake of smartphones. It is cheering in a way, but none of them come close.

A   Architects of the 2015 UN climate talks in Paris, France, (left to right, Christiana Figueres, Laurent Fabius, Ban Ki Moon and Francois Hollande) raise their hands to celebrate the historic agreement.

B   US Secretary of State John Kerry holds his granddaughter, Isabelle Dobbs-Higginson, as he signs the Paris Agreement, in the United Nations General Assembly Hall, April 2016.

C   Protesters gathered near the White House within minutes of President Donald Trump's announcement that he was withdrawing the United States from the Paris climate accord, June, 2017.

We are now in a position where we are trying to keep global warming to 1.5°C (2.7°F) with an exceptionally sharp deadline, all the time managing the impacts of the climate change we have already caused. We may well have to survive the best we can at 2°C (3.6°F), or higher, while fighting to stave off any further rise.

Scientists estimate we should hit the 1.5°C (2.7°F) marker sometime in the 2030s or 2040s, although it could be a little earlier, or a little later. We will not feel the impacts of this straight away. It takes a while for glaciers to melt and for sea levels to rise. Likewise, species extinctions and crop failure will most likely happen after repeated seasons of poor weather, and although the extra heat increases the risks of extreme weather events such as hurricanes, it is difficult to assess exactly when they will commence, or how hard people will be hit.

c

A world at 2°C (3.6°F) global warming is substantially more dangerous than one at 1.5°C (2.7°F). Just that half a degree on the Celsius scale is the difference between an ice-free summer in the Arctic every 100 years and one at least every 10, with insects and plants almost twice as likely to lose half their habitat.

There are significant differences when it comes to how many millions of people will be exposed to flooding and drought too. At 1.5°C (2.7°F), the global population exposed to flooding in coastal areas by the end of the century will be 60 million a year and the population exposed to severe drought will be 132.5 million. At 2°C (3.6°F) as many as 72 million people living in coastal areas will be exposed to flooding and the global population exposed to severe drought will rise to 194.5 million. The population exposed to severe heat increases significantly too. At 1.5°C (2.7°F), 14% of the population will face a severe heatwave at least every 5 years and 50% of the population will face one every 20 years, while at 2°C (3.6°F) the population affected rises to 27% and 70%, respectively.

A

A **carbon sink** is a natural system that sucks up and stores carbon dioxide from the atmosphere. Marine and terrestrial ecosystems, including trees, oceans and soils, currently sequester around 5.6 gigatons of carbon per year (i.e. about 60% of what we emit).

A   Severely drought-affected land in Coonabarabran, New South Wales, Australia. The 2018 drought there was the worst in living memory.
B   Local residents fill containers with drinking water from a municipal tanker in Kolkata, capital of India's West Bengal state.
C   A diver explores coral bleaching in French Polynesia. One of reasons for keeping to 1.5°C (2.7°F) warming is that beyond this, we would likely lose all coral reefs.

B

c

Between 2°C (3.6°F) and 3°C (5.4°F), we can expect the very last of the coral reefs to disappear, bringing a chain of species down with them. People who rely on these reefs will suffer, although by then they will have had several metres of sea level rise to contend with, so might have moved anyway. This could happen by the middle of this century, or earlier. We're already grazing 1°C (1.8°F).

The risk of reaching tipping points goes up after 2°C (3.6°F), too. Individual changes will impact on other parts of the climate system, causing irreversible, and sometimes unpredictable, damage and hastening the speed of global warming.

There's a point, for example, at which the Amazon rainforest could reach a level of no return, robbing us of not only its vital biodiversity, but also an essential carbon sink. Rainforests produce their own rain as plants lose water when they breathe. But increased levels of carbon dioxide mean that plants do not have to breathe so often, which means less water is released and the rainforest's supply of rain decreases. Add deforestation, wildfires and persistent drought from global warming and the rainforest dries up. Indeed, at some levels of destruction, the Amazon could start adding carbon to the atmosphere rather than help keep it out.

A

We could see tipping points in the Arctic too. Massive ice sheets in West Antarctica and Greenland could disintegrate irreversibly, condemning us to several more metres of sea-level rise for centuries to come. The Greenland ice cap alone contains enough water, were it to melt, to raise sea levels globally by around 7 metres (23 ft). More worryingly, the Arctic tundra contains large deposits of the oft-forgotten greenhouse gas methane, which could be released as it melts. Clathrates are currently kept in place by a mix of temperature and water pressure, but it is estimated that they contain twice as much energy as all the fossil fuels combined. Warm the Arctic enough and they could be released, emitting catastrophic quantities of methane in the process. This could all come sooner than expected. In summer 2019, an expedition in the Canadian Arctic found perma-frost outposts there thawing 70 years earlier than predicted.

Climate science is not a precise art. We do not know exactly what will happen at any given point, but we do know with very high levels of certainty that as the world warms, extreme weather events will get worse. The European heatwave in 2003, which killed 30,000 people, could become an annual event. Hurricane rainfall could increase by a third, while wind speeds could be boosted by as much as 13 metres per second (25 kn). After years and years of difficult weather conditions, crops will fail and many people will starve.

Those that can will move. Those than cannot will be left behind. There have been headlines about more than 140 million climate migrants by 2050. In truth, climate migration is hard to calculate because it is one of the many ways in which climate impacts will mix with our reaction to them. If we build flood defences and develop more drought-resistant crops, for example, the need for migration will be lower.

People will most likely move though, as will other species. The emergence of the 'pizzly' or 'grolar' bear, a cross between grizzly and polar bears, is a good example. The two species should not share habitats, but as sea ice melts, they are increasingly finding themselves in the same spaces, and mating. As the *Washington Post* headline put it drily: 'Love in the time of climate change.' A similar shifting of species could also have played a role in recent outbreaks of Ebola, as bat populations were forced to move, bringing the disease with them. The growth of mosquito-borne diseases, such as malaria, is especially worrying.

A   An iceberg that broke away from the Upsala glacier, part of the Southern Patagonian Ice Field, is seen floating in Lake Argentino from a tourist boat, April 2019.

B   Both polar and grizzly bears are shifting location as global warming changes their habitats, with 'pizzly' or 'grolar' bears being reported, the result of the two species mating.

C   Polar bears feeding at a garbage dump near the village of Belushya Guba, northern Russia. Conflicts with ice-dependent polar bears will increase as the Arctic ice melts.

Clathrates are icy, lattice-shaped chemical structures, sometimes known as 'the ice that burns', which contain gas under high pressure. When they come to the surface, the gas is released with a hiss and pop. If ignited, they burn.

B

C

The **World Health Organization (WHO)** is a specialized agency of the UN concerned with international public health. It was established in 1948, and its headquarters are in Geneva, Switzerland.

The **Clean Air Act** (1956) was passed in the UK after London's Great Smog of 1952. It included regulation of both domestic and industrial smoke emissions and introduced 'smoke control areas'.

A

B

A   Dry and polluting weather over the city of São Paulo, south east Brazil. Dry air makes it difficult to disperse pollutants, which impairs air quality in large urban centres.

B   Activists stage a 'die-in' in a protest over poor air quality in Paris, France, summer 2019. Public Health France believes air pollution in France is responsible for 48,000 premature deaths a year.

C   A woman wears a mask and filter in Beijing, China, December 2015. The Beijing government had just issued a 'red alert' with much of the city shrouded in heavy pollution.

If global warming creeps up to 3°C (5.4°F), 4°C (7.2°F) or even 5°C (9°F) or 6°C (10.8°F), we can expect more of the same to more extreme levels. There are more alarming tipping points then too. For example, at around 5°C (9°F) the carbon dioxide levels could get so high clouds might break up, so they no longer shade the surface, ratcheting global warming up to 8°C (14.4°F). Even at this point, there will most likely be humans on Earth, just fewer of them, living harder lives. What the hotter options might look like, and how close we are to them, depends on when we take more action and how climate pressures might combine with other problems. As earth systems scientist Myles Allen puts it: 'I don't think we'll make it to five degrees. I'm far more worried about geopolitical breakdown as the injustices of climate change emerge as we steam from two to three.'

For many, there are more immediate environmental crises than global warming. They cannot breathe.

According to the World Health Organization (WHO), around 91% of the world's population lives in places where air quality levels exceed safe limits. Every year, there are 4.2 million deaths caused by outdoor air pollution, with another 3.8 million due to household exposure.

The problem is partly caused by pollution from cars, trains and aeroplanes, but agriculture, mining and other industrial processes also contribute, as does the burning of fossil fuels directly in the home, which many people in the world still rely on for heat and light. It is an issue that affects countries both rich and poor, although as with any environmental problem, it is the people who are already struggling with other problems who are most at risk. London might have addressed its own coal habit years ago, eradicating its 'pea-soupers' with the Clean Air Act of 1956, but Londoners still rely on coal, in a way. Many of the products we carry around were produced by a coal-powered plant in another country. We have just offshored the problem to other peoples' lungs. In addition, the richer, coal-free cities continue to have issues with pollution: gushing, invisibly but violently out of the back end of most cars. Doctors also warn about the indoor pollution caused by cooking, deodorants and the fact that people are still opting for the aesthetic of an open fire, even when (unlike much of the rest of the world) they have an alternative.

c

Size matters in all of this. Your nose is pretty good at filtering out anything nasty you might breathe in. If you blow your nose and it is dirty, that is a sign that your body is protecting you. Unfortunately, smaller PM-tens and PM-twenty-fives – tiny particles capable of entering the bloodstream and penetrating deep into lung passageways – get through. These particles not only aggravate asthma and other breathing problems; they also affect our hearts and brains, resulting in more strokes, heart attacks, depression and dementia. Worldwide, outdoor air pollution accounts for 29% of all deaths and disease from lung cancer, 24% of all deaths from stroke and 43% of all deaths and disease from chronic obstructive pulmonary disease.

Poor air quality is part of the climate story, too. Numerous sources of air pollution, from coal plants to car engines, are also producers of high carbon dioxide emissions. Many of the key players in air pollution (ground level ozone and methane, for example) are also powerful greenhouse gases. Act on climate change, and we will all breathe easier.

A

PARTICULATE MATTER (PM 2.5) AIR POLLUTION (2016)
Population-weighted average level of exposure to concentrations of suspended particles measuring less than 2.5 microns in diameter. Exposure is measured in micrograms per cubic metre ($\mu g/m^3$)

| No data | 0 µg | 10 µg | 20 µg | 30 µg | 40 µg | 50 µg | 60 µg | 80 µg | 100 µg | 120 µg | >140 µg |

PM-tens and PM-twenty-fives are particles with a diameter of less than 10 microns (PM10), including fine particles of less than 2.5 microns (PM2.5).

Chronic obstructive pulmonary disease is the name for a group of lung conditions that cause breathing difficulties, for example emphysema and chronic bronchitis. Symptoms include breathlessness, a chesty cough with phlegm and wheezing.

B

C

Soot, or black carbon, is a particularly bad offender. As it works its way around the water cycle, through clouds and rain or snow, it can settle on top of ice, darkening its previously gleaming white reflective surfaces. Just as a black T-shirt gets hot on a sunny day, the darkened ice holds the heat, speeding up glacier retreat and thinning in mountainous regions and the Arctic.

To make matters worse, in the mountains between France and Spain, it is raining plastic. It might look like the same rain that has poured down for generations, but this is something different, something new and man-made.

That plastic has been polluting our waters is a well-established fact.

A

Well before politicians started making a show of carrying reusable coffee cups a couple of summers ago, oceanographers have been warning about piles of plastic trash. The Great Pacific Garbage Patch was discovered in 1997, and predicted by scientists as early as 1988. It was not until 2019 that plastic was found in rain and air though, in the seemingly pristine Pyrenees, 120 kilometres (75 mi) from a city.

A study in 2017 found microplastics in 83% of tap water samples globally, as plastic that is used and disposed of as drinks bottles, single-use contact lenses, microbeads in toothpaste and clothes degrades and makes its way into waterways. When water was sampled in the USA – from taps in places such as Congress buildings, the US Environmental Protection Agency's HQ or Trump Tower in New York – the figure was as high as 94%.

At least 8 million tonnes (8.8 million tons) of plastic end up in our oceans every year, making up 80% of all marine debris. Some researchers even refer to ocean plastic as our 'seventh continent'. Marine species ingest or get entangled in this plastic, resulting in injury or even death. According to the UN, marine plastic pollution has increased tenfold since 1980, affecting at least 267 species, including 86% of marine turtles, 44% of seabirds and 43% of marine mammals.

The **Great Pacific Garbage Patch**, also known as the Pacific trash vortex, is a collection of marine litter that spans waters from the west coast of North America to Japan.

Microplastics are small plastic pieces less than 5 mm (⅕ in.) long, either because they were made this small, or they have degraded.

Human-produced noise can be a problem too. Whales, fish and other marine life rely on a rich soundscape of rumbles, pops, chips, grunts, bubbles, knocks and clicks. Add our own noises into the mix – from ships, or sonar to explore for oil and gas – and you risk disrupting their ability to find food and mates or to avoid predators. Some blasts of noise can even directly kill marine life.

Humans also extract a lot from the oceans. We might have curtailed the whaling industry, but the number of overfished stocks has tripled globally in the past 50 years, with the UN classing about a third of the world's fisheries as being pushed to their limits. We extract oil and gas from the seabed, too, and some metals. As we deplete the easier-to-reach sources, industries are increasingly moving into new areas, including remote regions with fragile ecosystems and unique biodiversity, hence recent controversies about drilling the Arctic or Amazon Reef.

B

A An aerial view of deforestation in the Amazon from illegal mining in Peru, 2019. It is estimated that illegal gold mining has caused irreversible ecological damage to more than 11,000 ha (27,182 ac) of forest.

B A burned trunk in an illegally deforested area in Brazil, 2009. In 2019, the Brazilian government came under international criticism after reports that deforestation in Brazil's portion of the Amazon had soared to over 88%.

C Graphs showing the increasing use of grazing land (left) and cropland (right) from 1600. Trees felled to provide the land can significantly contribute to global warming and biodiversity loss.

The possible growth of deep-sea mining is particularly concerning, not least because the deep sea remains relatively understudied. There is so much about life there that we are yet to discover, which makes it hard for us to properly assess risks and work out how best to safeguard the environment. The desire to drill the deep sea is driven partly by the market for electronic devices, but also by materials needed for so-called 'clean energy', such as solar panels and batteries. Fossil fuels pose the largest threat to the health of the seas, but clean energy is not without its impacts. It is vital that large renewable energy infrastructure (offshore wind, for example) is responsibly sited.

We are having even more impact on land. Every second, more than 1 hectare (2.5 ac) of tropical forests is damaged or destroyed. Over half of the tropical forests worldwide have been destroyed since the 1960s, and a further 3.7 million hectares (9.1 million ac) of Europe's forests have been damaged by the actions of humans. In 2015, research estimated that 15 billion trees are cut down each year, and that the global number of trees has fallen 46% since the start of human civilization.

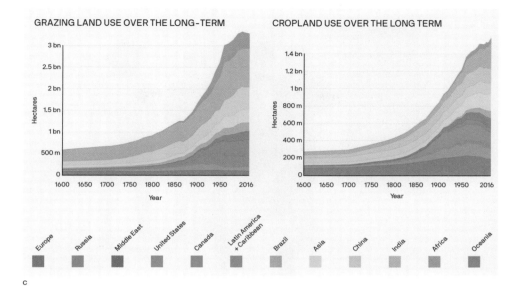

GRAZING LAND USE OVER THE LONG-TERM

CROPLAND USE OVER THE LONG TERM

Europe · Russia · Middle East · United States · Canada · Latin America + Caribbean · Brazil · Asia · China · India · Africa · Oceania

c

The UN estimates that more than 1.5 billion hectares (3.7 billion ac) of natural ecosystems has been converted to croplands, with crop or grazing lands now covering more than a third of the Earth's surface as we have cleared forests, grasslands and wetlands, including some of the most species-rich ecosystems on the planet.

The impact of this can be seen in the quality of the world's soil. A handful of dirt might not have the glamour and charisma of a polar bear, panda or any of the other endangered species highlighted by charities, but it is crucial to our survival. Half of the topsoil on the planet has been lost in the past 150 years, and the soil that remains is diminishing in quality, compromising our ability to grow food. Fertile soil is being lost at the rate of 24 billion tonnes (26.4 billion tons) a year, largely due to intensive farming.

A

A   Members of the Guardians
     of the Forest, an armed militia
     formed by the Guajajara
     tribe to protect the Araribóia
     Indigenous Reserve, Brazil,
     from loggers attempting
     to fell hardwood trees.
B   Marine scientists study the
     leatherback turtle, Florida,
     USA. Counting nests and
     eggs monitors the health
     of this endangered species.

The **Red List**, or the
Red List of Threatened
Species, was founded
in 1965 as a way
to keep track of
threatened species.
It provides criteria to
evaluate extinction risk
and also the world's
most comprehensive
inventory of the global
conservation status
of plant and animal
species.

Without vegetation to anchor
the soil, the earth can simply be
swept away. In addition to polluting
rivers and streams, degraded land
loses some of its ability to hold
water, thus increasing flood risks.
The breakdown of land can
have significant psychological
impacts, too. Land is identity
for many people, as our personal
surroundings shape memories,
traditions and beliefs. As soil is
lost, so too are sacred places and
rituals, traditional cultures, even
languages. In the process, we
also forfeit knowledge, including,
inevitably, techniques to manage
land that could have helped us
tackle the problems in the first
place. Research shows that
deforestation rates are two to
three times lower when forests are
managed by indigenous people.

These actions are hurting human health, and we are bringing down other species with us. More than 500,000 species have insufficient habitats for long-term survival. We could well be looking at driving more than 1 million to extinction.

According to the Red List, the proportion of species currently threatened with extinction averages around 25% across the many animal and plant groups, on land or in waters. This includes more than 40% of amphibian species, almost a third of reef-forming corals, sharks and shark relatives and more than a third of marine mammals. These statistics include only those which can be reliably counted. For all that we are brilliant at dominating the planet, we still have some catching up to do with regard to studying it. Much of nature still hides from our sight, even if it is increasingly difficult for it to hide from our impacts.

B

A

What is more, nature is becoming less diverse. When it comes to plants and animals that we have domesticated, we are losing whole varieties and breeds as we stick to an increasingly smaller set of options. This poses a serious risk to global food security, as a less diverse set of crops is more vulnerable to disease. It also limits our ability to develop new crops that might be more resilient to climate change.

And then there are the bees. Beekeepers have long known that bees sometimes disappear. A so-called 'disappearing disease' has been recorded since the mid-19th century; periodically, the bulk of worker bees disappear, leaving behind their queen. But this was a reasonably rare occurrence. Then, in the winter of 2006–07, beekeepers in the mid-Atlantic and Pacific Northwest reported bees disappearing at alarmingly high rates. The phenomenon was renamed Colony Collapse Disorder and environmental campaigners, scientists and policy-makers around the world started to explore why it was happening.

In October 2017, headlines warning of an 'insect apocalypse' started to appear all over the Internet: a loss of three-quarters of insects was claimed, threatening the entire collapse of nature. This was a slight overstatement. Researchers had looked at data from insect traps in 63 different nature reserves in Germany over a 27-year period. The weight of insects they were collecting had dropped by a terrifying 77%. This was incredibly concerning, but not the same as all insect populations, everywhere, dropping to a quarter of what they were. The UN report of May 2019 suggests what the data highlight is a conservative estimate of 10% of insect species threatened with extinction.

The sheer diversity of insects makes them incredibly difficult to study. There are more species of ladybirds than mammals, for example. There are more types of weevil than fish. So far, scientists have managed to describe about 1 million insect species, but there are so many more they have not yet logged. And it is hard to measure something you have not identified. Reports of the death of insects might well have been overstated, but that does not mean we should not be worried. Some 75% of food crop types rely on animal pollination, including coffee and chocolate, which are vital to some economies.

A   Workers hang freshly harvested banana bunches in Ecuador, one of the world's largest banana exporters. Although over a thousand species of banana have been recorded in the wild, most sold in the West belong to same subgroup of the species, and are nearly identical genetically. This makes them highly vulnerable to disease.

B   Beehives before and after colony collapse disorder. In the winter of 2006–07, beekeepers in the mid-Atlantic and Pacific Northwest US reported bees disappearing at alarmingly high rates. Over a decade on, it is clear bees in the US are still struggling, but less so than before, and they appear to be doing better in other parts of the world, such as Europe.

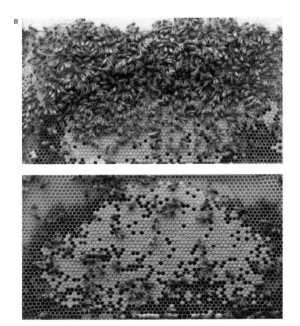

B

Did we sleepwalk into all this environmental damage? It is a tempting thesis, but rather a questionable one.

Slogans such as 'Exxon Knew' and 'Shell Knew' have become familiar refrains of environmentalist campaigns in the past few years, pointing to various internal reports in the 1970s and 1980s. But climate change was never hidden from the general population. James Hansen (b. 1941) famously warned Congress about climate change in 1985, and this was widely covered by the mainstream press. Moreover, he was not the first, by a long way. Roger Revelle (1909–91) was briefing politicians in DC on global warming in the 1950s. Lots of people knew.

As far back as 1856, US scientist Eunice Foote (1819–88), experimenting with how the sun's rays interact with different gases, wrote: 'An atmosphere of that gas [carbon dioxide] would give to our Earth a high temperature.' She was largely ignored, possibly because she was a woman. When her research was published in a scientific magazine, it was under the rather dismissive title 'Scientific Ladies'. Similar research was undertaken by Irish physicist John Tyndall (1820–93) a few years later and presented at the Royal Institution in London, UK, in 1859 at an event chaired by Prince Albert. When he published his book on heat in 1863, it was a best seller. Climate change is not a small bit of hidden science. It has been part of the mainstream for more than 150 years.

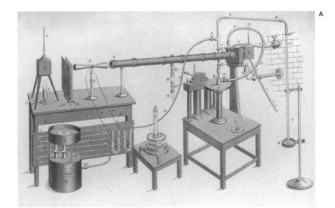

A

Eugenics is a philosophy aiming to engineer the human population by promoting particular genetic groups above others. The modern understanding is often seen as linked to white supremacism.

A   John Tyndall's apparatus for measuring the heat absorption of gases. Tyndall experimented with a range of gases he thought could be in the atmosphere, establishing in the 1850s that both water vapour and carbon are what today we would call greenhouse gases.

B   John Tyndall lecturing at the Royal Institution, London, UK, 1870. Sadly, there is not a photograph of Eunice Foote on record. She was wealthy enough that one might have been made during her lifetime, even if history temporarily allowed her to be forgotten, and historians hope to find one soon.

B

Also in the 19th century, German philosopher Friedrich Engels (1820–95) warned of the environmental impacts of capitalism, critiquing the short-term thinking of Spanish coffee planters in Cuba who burnt forests to fertilize crops. Further back, there is the British philosopher Thomas Robert Malthus (1766–1834), who taught at the East India Company's college. Malthus argued against more utopian thinking of the time, believing any improvements in society would only increase population and thus also the number of mouths to feed. He maintained that some of the population at least would inevitably be pulled back into poverty as conditions got better. Malthus's ideas have continued to be extremely influential, although controversial. You can trace them through the history of eugenics, including the influence this had on both family planning and conservation movements.

Without doubt, it is time for us to take greater responsibility. We know we hold power, so how can we use it well? How can we shape human behaviour to benefit the planet? Chapters 3 and 4 will explore the options we have for positive change.

3. The Techno-fix

It is tempting to blame technology for the current state of the environment, but technology, done well, is the best of humanity. It reflects our creativity and ability to share ideas and work together. Technologies can and will play a role in us surviving the Anthropocene.

We should be wary of techno-fixes that do not sufficiently consider the new risks they might pose, especially when it comes to environmental problems. But to put technology in opposition to what is natural, good or human is a highly reactionary perspective.

A

A Entrance to the
Svalbard seed vault,
1,300 km (808 miles)
from the North Pole.
This long-term
seed storage facility
opened in 2008
to preserve a wide
variety of plant
seeds and to insure
against the loss of
seeds held in other
banks worldwide.
B Wind turbine blades
await transport at
a production facility
in Iowa, USA.

As philosopher Donna Haraway says: 'I'd rather be a cyborg than a goddess': it is better to live a life full of the power and compromises that come from assimilating ourselves with machines and other people than imagine that it is possible to exist in some ideal of purity.

Rather than being pro or anti technology, we need to be critical about the options on offer, and ask which technology, who owns it and why? We should also question whether we really need that particular technology, because the 'genie out of the bottle' view – once a technology is developed we cannot stop it – is just not true. We routinely turn our backs on technologies: whale oil as a lubricant for car engines, Betamax, typewriters and lesser known technologies that never made their way to market, for example.

When it comes to tackling our various environmental problems, we have a range of technological options on offer.

B

A   Volunteers use green construction techniques to rebuild a self-managed social centre in Rome, Italy, after it was destroyed by a fire in 2012. The final project will be highly energy efficient, as well as standing up to fire and earthquakes.

B   Journalists tour a 22 square metre (26 sq yard) 'tiny house' in New York, USA. The module was designed to spark public debate over eco design. Some critics have pushed against the idea that sustainable living must be small, not least because less storage space can lead to greater use of disposable products.

C   A gas meter (left) and new smart electricity meter (right). Alongside efforts to clean up our electricity and gas supplies, we will also need to greatly reduce our use of domestic energy. Digitization of the process, which allows us to better target when and where we light or heat rooms, for example, should help us to do so.

Firstly, if we want to cut carbon emissions, we can simply consume less energy. This is partly a matter of choosing not to use some technologies (cars, aircraft, for example), but it also involves technological development in itself: more efficient machines, better buildings, etc.

Energy efficiency is sometimes dubbed the 'Cinderella' of environmental action because it is so often ignored. It can offer a rare good news story, though. A study of British emissions by environmental analysis website Carbon Brief in January 2019 found that British electricity demand had fallen to the level it was in 1994, in part due to the introduction of European Union (EU) product standards on vacuum cleaners and other appliances, as well as innovations such as LED light bulbs and shifts made by industry, for example supermarket chains improving their refrigeration systems.

This progress is nowhere near enough, but it is going in the right direction.

Quietly transforming household appliances without people noticing is not necessarily the best idea in the long term. If technologies are coming into our homes, arguably we should have more involvement with what they do and whom they serve. One of the next big steps in energy efficiency – and the energy industry in general – is the increase of digitization, including technologies for smarter homes that will record which devices we are using, and when. Some customers may be happy to swap privacy for cheaper bills and greener energy; others will be suspicious. There have already been headlines about refrigerators spying on us, and we could well see a backlash against smart homes that could, in turn, slow climate action. Or we might find more open and democratic ways to build data-driven improvements to our energy systems.

However we choose to do it, cutting energy use will reduce carbon emissions, but only to a certain extent. We also need to electrify as much of our energy as possible, and then create that electricity using low carbon sources such as renewables and nuclear energy.

c

A

The UN likes to talk breezily about the unstoppable rise of wind and solar power, but a large amount of the electricity we consume is still produced using fossil fuels. According to the app on my phone, the national grid I am working off is about 55% low carbon right now. That is unusually clean; it is a very windy day. Still, electricity gives us the option to generate energy via low carbon methods in ways that a petroleum-powered car or gas fire do not.

The growth of wind and solar power grabs headlines, but hydropower is one of the most established renewable energy sources. Geothermal power is key in some parts of the world, and tidal could be too, if it were given some strategic investment. It is also worth remembering that within the categories of wind and solar power sits a range of different technologies, and there is an increasing divide between the massive machines generating offshore wind power and smaller onshore wind farms, just as there is a difference between rooftop solar panels and larger solar farms.

Geothermal energy, more colourfully known as volcano power, uses heat from the Earth itself. We have used hot springs to heat homes since Roman times and to generate electricity since the early 20th century.

Tidal energy is a form of hydropower that converts the energy obtained from tides into useful forms of power, mainly electricity. It is not yet widely used, and developmental costs coupled with some environmental concerns make it controversial. However, it has a lot of potential for future electricity generation.

Natural gas, not to be confused with gasoline, is a fossil fuel alongside oil and coal. Coal gas – or town gas – is produced by burning coal, and was produced before natural gas could be transported easily.

Britain's electricity grid is doing a sterling job of quitting coal, and the Netherlands seems to be making movements towards ditching natural gas. China has been installing wind turbines at the rate of one an hour. Still, it is questionable whether any of this progress is fast enough. We are adding renewables to grids all over the world at unprecedented rates, but as the IPCC's Global Warming of 1.5°C report makes very clear, we have to do better than 'unprecedented'. Any other major transitions humans have managed previously look tiny next to the scale of what is needed.

It is also important to remember that all energy production methods leave their mark.

Wind and solar farms require building materials. The impact of lithium, used in batteries to store renewable energy (in a solar-powered car, for example), is especially significant and could grow as both an environmental and human rights concern. Hydro is as controversial as nuclear for some environmentalists because of its impact on wildlife, and although the role of wind turbines as bird killers is often overstated, they can hurt bird populations if not situated well. There is also the question of land. This isn't just a matter of people complaining turbines spoil the view from their golf courses. In Western Sahara, wind and solar installations on contested land have led to accusations of using renewable energy to further colonialism.

Colonialism via renewable energy: a very 21st-century problem.

Even if we could turn the grid green, not everything is easily electrified. You can already switch to an electric car or catch an electric double decker bus, and manufacturers of trucks and ships are starting to make substantial moves into this market. However, we are still far from fully electrifying land and sea transport and a very long way from electrifying domestic air flight.

The **International Energy Agency (IEA)** was established in 1974 in the wake of the 1973 oil crisis and reports regularly on energy trends. It is headquartered in Paris, France.

A   Two electric filling stations in an underground car park, Bavaria, Germany. Car parks full of electric cars can also offer battery storage options as we shift to renewables.

B   It might not be the slickest design, but this self-built solar car was cobbled together by its owner in Xiqing district, China, in 2016 to provoke environmental awareness.

C   So-called 'trackless trams' which are fully electric and run on virtual train lines, in Zhuzhou, China, 2018. No requirement for tracks makes installation far less disruptive.

c

A few years ago, there was a flurry of attention when a solar plane attempted a trip around the world in the run-up to the UN climate talks in 2015. A privately financed project led by engineer and businessman André Borschberg (b. 1952) and psychiatrist and balloonist Bertrand Piccard (b. 1958), the aim was for the plane to leave Abu Dhabi in March 2015 and return the following August. By July, the aircraft's batteries had been damaged on the leg between Japan and Hawaii. After several months' delay, the flight resumed in April 2016 and, after a few stops, returned to its starting point in July 2016, a little more than 16 months after it had first taken off. It was an amazing project, but clearly we are still a long way from using solar planes to take us to our holiday destinations. Indeed, it could be argued that such projects are merely a PR distraction from the cultural change that is needed to reduce flying per se.

Moreover, although the recent rise of the electric car has been a genuine success story, progress is not moving fast enough. The International Energy Agency (IEA) estimates that there were 3.1 million electric vehicles in 2017, and this could rise to 125 million by 2030. That sounds incredible. But there are 1 billion motor vehicles in the world, so we are only talking a bit over 10%.

A A burger wrapped in edible packaging. As a stunt for Earth Day 2018, New Zealand-owned chain Better Burger challenged their customers to eat everything on their plate, including the packaging.

B New York anti-packaging activist Lauren Singer displays all the non-recyclable and non-compostable waste she has generated over five years. Collectively, it fits into a 450-gram (16-oz) jar. Singer is an exception; many of us would generate more than this in just a few hours.

Materials science also has to be part of our arsenal. This can help us with energy efficiency, and so much more. So-called 'plyscrapers' (plywood skyscrapers), for example, are popping up around the world, for instance in Norway, Canada, Japan and New Zealand. Using a type of engineered timber made by gluing layers of low-grade plywood together, they provide one option for reducing our addiction to cement.

There are various interesting approaches to solving the plastic waste problem too. Edible, plant-based pods filled with isotonic drinks were handed out at the London marathon in 2019 instead of single use plastic water bottles. Make packaging out of mushrooms and it will rot more easily. Looking at the problem from another direction, in 2016, Japanese researchers found a bacteria living in a waste dump that seemed to have evolved to eat plastic, able to break down the molecular bonds of polyethylene terephthalate (PET, one of the world's most common plastics). The race is now on to tweak the enzyme so it can be used to recycle plastics more effectively.

We can also improve product design: build products for reuse and repair, not replacement, and develop infrastructure for reusable packaging so we do not produce so much waste in the first place. We could use modular phones, for example, where parts can be repaired or upgraded without needing to throw away the whole device, or visit zero-waste shops. One firm thinks it might have a solution to palm oil based on reusing old coffee grounds. As we will discuss in Chapter 4, simply banning palm oil is not a good idea, so this could be a sustainable alternative.

B

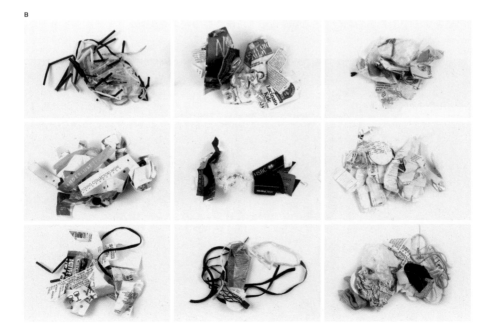

A   An experiment in
    'speed-breeding'
    barley seedlings
    at the University of
    Queensland, Australia.
    Based on NASA
    techniques developed
    for growing plants in
    space, researchers grow
    plants in a greenhouse
    where the lights are kept
    on for 22 hours a day.
B   Proposed branding for
    Super Meat, a company
    promising to develop
    'meal-ready' meat from
    animal cells grown in a
    lab. Such 'clean meat'
    promises meat without
    animal slaughter and,
    potentially, much lower
    environmental impact.

If we are going to save the planet, we require more of this sort of circular economy thinking.

We may well need biological engineering, too. For example, Joanne Chory (b. 1955), a plant biologist at the Salk Institute in San Diego, USA, is leading a project on the use of gene editing – via traditional horticulture and CRISPR – to grow plants with bigger, deeper roots that will collect more carbon dioxide. Techniques like these could also be used to produce crops that do not need so many pesticides, or can more readily stand up to the pressures of a changing climate.

Lab-grown meat is one way to tackle climate change and other issues surrounding the use of land for farming without relying on people to change their diets. It remains eye-wateringly expensive, though, and has perhaps been beaten by the lower tech idea of heme, or even beetroot dye coupled with inventive use of soya. Methane from cows' digestion is part of the greenhouse gas problem, and there is also a fair bit of research into vaccinating cows so they burp less.

A

But maybe this is all just tinkering at the margins. Why do we not go big and suck carbon dioxide out of the atmosphere?

It is worth knowing that when the IPCC says it is possible to keep to an upper limit of 1.5°C (2.7°F) global warming, there is an assumption that negative emissions technologies will be part of the plan, thus putting this technology alongside a radical transition to low-carbon energy.

Circular economy is a regenerative alternative to the traditional linear economy that throws away goods after they have been used once. In a circular economy, we keep and reuse products for as long as possible and then, when their useful life ends, we recover and regenerate their materials.

CRISPR – Clustered Regularly Interspaced Short Palindromic Repeat – is a relatively new technique that offers scientists powerful new ways to precisely target and cut genetic material.

Heme is an iron-containing compound that is added to some meatless burgers to create a meaty flavour.

Negative emissions technologies, sometimes abbreviated to NETs, are a very broad range of technologies that remove carbon dioxide from the atmosphere. Some work via photosynthesis (at its most simple, a tree, but it is rarely that simple); others are based on geochemistry or chemical engineering.

A

So-called 'direct air capture' (DAC) technologies are still at the early stages of development, but there are several companies taking them seriously. In fact, you might already have consumed cola containing bubbles produced via this technology. Although DAC is very expensive, costs are dropping rapidly: US research argues that the cost of removing 1 tonne (1.1 tons) of carbon dioxide has fallen from $232 to $94 between 2011 and 2018. The idea is to remove carbon dioxide from the atmosphere and turn it into something more useful. As well as providing the bubbles for fizzy drinks, we could potentially turn it into fuel. By mixing carbon dioxide with hydrogen and electricity, you can produce synthetic hydrogen-based fuels, which would be an amazing alternative to oil and gas – as long as the electricity is renewable (from offshore wind, for example), the hydrogen comes from solar-powered electrolysis and the carbon dioxide is from DAC.

A Some Climeworks direct air capture equipment. The company has even started marketing to individuals. For €7 a month, they will turn 85 kg (187 lb) of CO_2 into stone in your name.
B Workers at the Hellisheidi geothermal power plant, near Reykjavik, Iceland – the world's first carbon negative power plant – inject CO_2 dissolved in water into the unique type of basaltic rock that surrounds the plant.
C An engineer at a direct air capture plant in Squamish, Canada, explains how their plant extracts carbon dioxide from the atmosphere and, after liquefying it, transforms it into solid pellets.

B

C

DAC is sometimes painted as the great hope of the fossil fuel industry, a technology that allows us to get away with burning more. Many environmentalists worry about it for this very reason: is gee-whiz rhetoric about a cool new technology being used to distract us from emissions cuts we urgently need to make? As David Keith (b. 1963), a climate physicist at Harvard who also heads up a DAC firm in Calgary, Canada, told *Nature* in 2015: 'Air capture has been stuck in a catfight between one group of people saying it is a silver bullet and one group saying it is bullshit. The truth is it is neither.' DAC is an exciting approach, one of many we should invest in learning more about, but it is no saviour and will only ever be part of a smorgasbord of options.

In order to reduce the amount of carbon dioxide in the atmosphere, we could increase the efficiency of our tree planting efforts. Forests are powerful carbon sinks, absorbing 2.4 billion tonnes (2.6 billion tons) of carbon dioxide a year. Could we just grow more trees?

China has planted more than 35 billion trees across 12 provinces as part of a $100-billion afforestation programme, absorbing 774 million tonnes (853 million tons) of carbon in the 30 years running up to 2003 alone. There have also been substantial investments into afforestation in the USA, although this has been driven either by charities or states working to bring new life to former mining areas.

Launched in 2014 as part of the Bonn Challenge, Pakistan's 'one billion tree tsunami' was completed in August 2017, ahead of schedule. In September 2018, its prime minister, Imran Khan (b. 1952), decided to venture further and plant 10 billion trees in just five years. Running across several countries in Africa, there is the dazzlingly ambitious Great Green Wall project, which aims to grow a wall of forest stretching across the width of the entire continent, just south of the Sahara.

A

B

Afforestation refers to the creation of new forests where there were none previously. It is slightly different to reforestation, in which trees that have, for whatever reason, died are replaced.

The **Bonn Challenge** was first developed in Germany in 2011 and later endorsed by the 2014 UN climate summit. 56 countries have pledged to restore 350 million hectares (865 million ac) of forest by 2030.

A   A Brazilian Air Force
    officer launches seeds
    of the andiroba tree from
    a military plane over a
    deforested area of the
    Amazon River basin,
    summer 2007.
B   Tree planting in Iceland.
    Before Vikings landed
    in Iceland in the late 9th
    century, it was lush with
    forests, but today it is
    the least forested country
    in Europe.
C   An aerial view of erosion
    control works in Turkey.
    Crews have been planting
    hundreds of thousands
    of trees to prevent further
    erosion in highland
    mountains and hills.

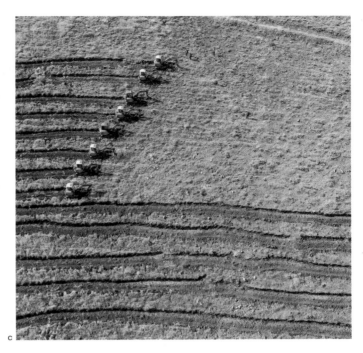

C

Planting trees might not seem like a technology, but afforestation at the scale we are talking about is best considered as such. We are doing something with natural forces, applying science to better our lives. It is imperative that this is done well. We should consider nature-based solutions as critically as more overtly mechanical technologies. Patchworks of green fields for farming, for example, are far from natural, and arguably highly damaging, as they take land from forests.

Like any approach for surviving the Anthropocene, forests come with a host of social, economic and environmental impacts. Many of these are positive and they can be managed. In addition to carbon dioxide absorption, tree planting can boost biodiversity, provide flood defences and fight land degradation, as the trees help anchor and restore soils. One of the purposes of the Great Green Wall project is to fight desertification. However, planting trees can also have devastating ecological impacts: for example, those caused by the production of palm oil, as discussed previously. It will also take a vast amount of fertilizer to plant all these trees, which in turn will have an environmental impact, including on greenhouse gas emissions. Indeed, this is one of the reasons why we might want to apply CRISPR techniques, to produce plants that need fewer chemicals to grow.

A

If we want to go a step further, there is rewilding: not just planting trees, but restoring wilderness to parts of the world we have cleared, including reintroducing plant and animal species and thus offering a boost to biodiversity. Some people even believe that one day we could bring back species that have become extinct.

A   Two wolves in the Czech Republic. Wolves in Europe have been subject to organized extermination efforts since the Middle Ages, but a mix of EU and national policies mean they can now be found in every European country besides the UK.

B   As this graph shows, even if we can rely on a lot of land-use change and negative emissions from BECCS, we will still need to drastically cut our fossil fuels to stick to 1.5°C (2.7°F).

Whether rewilding is included or not, if we want to counteract all the carbon dioxide we pump out, we would need to plant an enormous number of trees. When Britain's Committee on Climate Change reported in November 2018 that land was needed for trees rather than grazing livestock, and so people might need to rethink their meat consumption, it was met with screams of pain that scientists had designs on the British roast dinner. Arguably, such protestations are misplaced, but getting the public onside is no small issue. At the sharper end of things are concerns that food prices will rise for those who are already struggling to feed themselves, or that greengrabbing, in which marginalized communities are pushed out to make way for global green projects, will proliferate.

Rewilding was first coined as a term by conservationist and radical activist Dave Foreman in the 1990s, although the basic idea is a lot older. It simply means restoring the lost richness of nature, an attempt to undo the damage of humankind.

Greengrabbing is a term first used by journalist John Vidal in the 2000s to name the appropriation of land and resources for environmental ends.

We might also be under pressure to use land to grow fuel. One of the more mature negative emissions technologies is bioenergy with carbon capture and storage, or BECCS. In this, trees or other plants that absorb carbon dioxide from the atmosphere are grown and then burnt in power stations to create electricity; the trick is that you also capture the emissions and store them underground. Although the technology works, it is expensive, does not produce much energy and still creates some pollutants. Additionally, if you want to operate on a reasonable scale you need to plant a lot of trees, thus using up a lot of land.

Together with trees, we should look to the 'blue lungs' of the planet, the ocean, which also takes a good share of carbon sequestration.

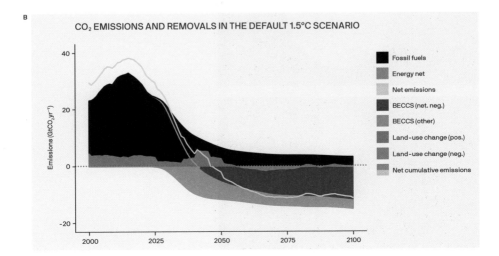

B

CO₂ EMISSIONS AND REMOVALS IN THE DEFAULT 1.5°C SCENARIO

Emissions (GtCO₂ yr⁻¹)

- Fossil fuels
- Energy net
- Net emissions
- BECCS (net. neg.)
- BECCS (other)
- Land-use change (pos.)
- Land-use change (neg.)
- Net cumulative emissions

A Pteropods, or 'sea
   butterflies', are found in
   all major oceans. These
   pteropod shells were
   exposed to seawater at pH
   levels projected for the year
   2100. After a month and a
   half, the shell had almost
   completely dissolved.
B The Earth's 'atmospheric
   limb' captured by the
   International Space Station,
   allowing us to see the
   different layers of the
   atmosphere that separate
   us from space.

For example, to rebalance the ocean acidification we have caused, we could grind up, disperse and dissolve alkaline rocks such as limestone. We could also feed iron, urea or volcanic ash into the oceans to boost populations of phytoplankton: these single-celled algae capture carbon dioxide via photosynthesis and then draw it deep into the ocean as they die (a sort of natural version of BECCS). Small-scale operations would not be adequate though; we are not talking about a few rocks or a sprinkle of ash. To remove 1 billion tonnes (1.1 billion tons) of carbon dioxide from the atmosphere (the ocean does more than 20 times this a day already), for example, would require roughly 2.5 billion tonnes (2.75 billion tons) of limestone. This would soon pile up, causing problems in itself.

Negative emissions technologies are sometimes lumped together with more controversial solar radiation management (SRM) technologies, under a larger banner of geoengineering.

A

Ocean acidification is sometimes called 'climate change's evil twin', and is another impact of all the carbon dioxide we are emitting. The ocean absorbs about 22 million tonnes (24 million tons) of carbon a day, before it even gets to the atmosphere, and this is drastically increasing its acidity.

Solar radiation management (SRM) is a diverse set of technologies aimed at limiting the effect of sunlight on the Earth.

B

One of the most talked about SRM technologies is aerosol injection. This technology replicates the effect of a volcanic eruption. When a volcano erupts, the sulphur dioxide in its ash cloud combines with water to form sulfuric acid aerosols and these can form clouds that reflect sunlight. Some strategically placed sunshine-reflecting clouds could be useful as things heat up in the 2030s. They could be used to ease extreme weather events such as heat waves or especially cold nights, for example, and could also bring rainfall back up to pre-industrial levels. But they might increase rainfall in some areas and decrease it in others, leaving some land too dry.

There is also the potential long-term effect of termination shock, in which the atmosphere becomes so reliant on SRM treatment that if it were stopped suddenly, the atmosphere would react badly, sending global temperatures rapidly rebounding. From a villainous perspective, this is great: get the planet hooked on aerosols, then blackmail world governments to keep paying for it to continue. But there is also the risk of political or terrorist attack. Given that we cannot seem to manage the more basic global political work of cutting our carbon, it does not seem like the sort of environmental risk set-up for which we have the global governance.

A

B

A Workers cover a
glacier on the peak
of Germany's highest
mountain, Zugspitze,
with oversized plastic
sheets intended to
keep the glacier from
melting during the
summer months.
B An artist's rendering
of how giant mirrors
might be placed in
space to act as a sort
of giant sunshade and
reflect solar radiation
away from the Earth.
C Streaky, crisscrossing
clouds like these are
found throughout
the world's oceans.
When first spotted
in 1965, researchers
wondered if they were
caused by aircraft,
or natural patterns of
air circulation, before
realizing they were
the exhausts of ships.
D An artist's impression
of what an unmanned,
cloud-generating ship
might look like.

Albedo, derived
from the Latin
for 'whiteness',
is a measure
of the ability of
astronomical
bodies (like
the Earth) to
reflect the sun's
radiation.

Other SRM technologies look at ways to increase the Earth's albedo. As discussed previously, black carbon is dimming the ice sheets' ability to reflect light, speeding up their warming in the same way that dark clothes worn on a sunny day make us feel hot. We could do the opposite. In hot countries, we already paint buildings white to reflect the sun. The roofs of some buses are also painted white for the same reason. We could lay reflective sheets in deserts or churn up the surfaces of oceans to make foam, which is more reflective than a bubble-free surface. The latter has the benefit of being easy to shut down: you just burst the bubbles. But it could still negatively impact marine ecosystems that rely on sunlight getting through, and to create the sea foam would require a lot of energy. Possibly the least disruptive option to life on Earth would be to place mirrors in space. However, the size that the mirrors would have to be might make them prohibitively expensive.

C

D

Alternatively, we could make clouds brighter by spraying salt water into them. In theory, we could target specific areas of cloud: for example, cooling an area over a coral reef, or a spot in the ocean that would help stop hurricanes from building up too much strength. Such action might also disrupt weather and biology, albeit on a local level. The thin, wispy cirrus clouds that form at high altitudes absorb a large amount of radiation, so even though they also reflect a little sunlight, overall they heat the planet more than humans. Another idea is to remove such clouds, using drones to spray them with desert dust. Unfortunately, there is a risk that this would lead to the formation of thicker, more persistent cirrus clouds.

Back in 2008, Greenpeace's Doug Parr described geoengineering as 'an expression of political despair': it is what you do when you have given up on all the other options. As we are not currently exploiting these options (basic investment in loft insulation, for example), geoengineering could seem rather ridiculous, a dangerous distraction even. Still, some scientists and policymakers consider it worth researching, even if they also hope we will never need it. In spring 2019, for example, the University of Cambridge, UK, announced it would be opening a new Centre for Climate Repair, to be coordinated by the British government's former chief scientific adviser, Sir David King (b. 1939). This will investigate, among other projects, ways to turn captured carbon dioxide into fuel, and to possibly refreeze the poles to brighten clouds above them. If we are wise, we will use the multitude of options on offer before we will ever need to reach for the cloud-brightening spray. But we might not be that smart.

If we are going to embrace geoengineering, we should at least do it well.

A

A A 'no to chemtrails' sticker, based on an old anti-nuclear power sticker of similar design. Chemtrail conspiracy theories have been circulating since the mid 1990s and are often directed at geoengineering discussions. Chemtrail believers see the contrails left by aircraft as evidence that governments are dispersing chemicals for weather modification, psychological manipulation, human population control or biological or chemical warfare.
B Officials seed clouds over fields just south of Bangkok, Thailand, 2007. During Thailand's dry season, these planes shovel salt into any clouds they can find, hoping to induce rain to clear away thick smoke from forest fires and stubble burning.

B

In summer 2018, a group of scientists and policymakers from the global south published a letter in *Nature* arguing that developing countries were going to be most affected by future climate change and should therefore play a central role in geoengineering research, discussion and evaluation. This follows the 'Oxford principles' of 2009, which argued that any geoengineering project should be regulated as a public good, that there should be public participation in decision-making wherever possible, that we need open publication of research results, that there should be independent assessment of impact, and that we need to work out our governance systems before we actually deploy anything.

Environmentalists can, on occasion, be wary of discussing technologies that could protect us from the impacts of climate change. A little like carbon capture, it can seem defeatist to talk about ways to adapt to a warmer world, as if we have given up on the idea of decarbonizing. But the truth is that climate change is already happening, and 21st-century approaches to saving the planet must think about both adaptation and mitigation.

A Concrete development in China and other countries around the world tends to block the natural flow of water. So-called 'sponge city' projects in China aim to reverse this, with urban design that aims to work with and absorb water rather than be flooded by it.
B An excavator lifts fortifying concrete blocks during dyke renovation work being carried out on the Wadden Sea coastline. Floods have always been a problem for the low-lying Netherlands.

A

As previously discussed, nature-based solutions such as tree planting can provide some support against flooding and help cool over-heated areas. It is also one of the reasons why biotech might be useful, too, helping us develop plants that can withstand different weather patterns. But we will also need flood defences, and buildings that are more able to stand up to changes in temperature, flooding and extreme winds. China is investing in a network of 'sponge cities', where concrete is replaced with wetlands, pavements are made more permeable, and rooftops are turned green with gardens so human infrastructure can work with water rather than be endangered by it.

The problem of adaption, however, is often less a matter of new technology and more to do with finance.

Much of the coastline of the Netherlands, for example, is protected by a dyke system, but this sort of infrastructure requires very large sums of money (both for construction and maintenance), which many countries do not have to spare. Even within richer countries, there can be a paucity of political will. In Britain, tens of thousands of people die every year from the effects of cold homes, something we could easily remedy with more investment in insulation and tighter building regulations.

There is no single 'silver bullet' technology that will solve the problem of global warming and reducing biodiversity, nor can technological options ever be effective without a host of political, cultural and economic work to support them. We have to be careful about the technologies we choose to apply, and remember that sometimes one of the cleverest things we can do with technology is to decide not to use it. But downing tools altogether is probably a bad idea.

B

A

A

A The Ouarzazate solar power station in the Drâa-Tafilalet region in Morocco. The world's largest concentrated solar plant, when completed, should produce over 500MW. The project has been criticized as an example of 'greengrabbing' land for low-carbon tech (appropriating land or resources for environmental ends).

B Large fleece blankets used to cover parts of the Rhone glacier in Switzerland in an attempt to stall the melting of the ice.

We should be critical and also enthusiastic about technology, and pick our technologies with a dose of political strategy: consider who owns it, who it helps and who it might hurt. We should think hard about which technology we want to turn our backs on, and which we want to invest our resources in.

Technology is part of what makes us human; it is also part of how we socialize and work together.

B

At its best, technology is a wonderful expression of the power of people to work collectively, drawing on materials and expertise from across continents and generations: so much more than the sum of its parts. It is how we do technology that matters, noting who is in control, and how we best ensure we minimize risk.

If none of these technologies appeal, there is always the techno-fix offered at the end of *Ten Billion* (2013), a book on environmental catastrophe by Microsoft researcher Stephen Emmott (b. 1960): protect yourself and get a gun.

4. Political Solutions

It is safe to say that we need to change rapidly, and on an unprecedented scale, in order to prevent further damage to our planet. Any revolution humans have managed previously – agricultural, scientific, economic, political, technological – pales into insignificance compared to the enormity of the challenge ahead.

Change at the scale we need is going to be disruptive, and some people may get hurt in the process, not least because it is likely jobs will be lost. Without effective programmes for retraining and reemployment, whole communities could be left destitute. British coal mines were not closed for environmental reasons in the 1980s, but the fallout from these closures offers a powerful warning of how not to handle industrial change. Some 30 years after most mines were shut, a 2014 study from the University of Sheffield, UK, showed the ongoing impact of the sudden job losses: particularly with regard to unemployment and health. The number of people living in these former mining communities is around 5.5 million, a little larger than the population of Scotland.

A

Filling plastic bottles with drinking water at the village of Shishkin Les, Russia. Bottled spa waters have been sold since the 18th century, and in the early 1970s, the development of polyethylene terephthalate (PET) meant plastic bottles could withstand the pressure of carbonated liquids.

B A Bangladeshi child works in a plastic bottle recycling factory in Dhaka, stripping off non-recyclable materials ready for sorting. Bangladesh is one of several countries that have increased their imports of western plastic waste after China closed its doors in 2017.

It is vital we transition to a low-carbon society quickly, but we must do so as fairly as possible.

The good news is that while we have been building roads, plastic bottle factories and ever-deeper oil wells, we have also constructed a plethora of social, cultural and political spaces within which environmental action can be taken. We have created levers for change, and we can create more.

B

The UN has created a range of environmental bodies, several of which have been mentioned in previous chapters. In 1972, the UN general assembly convened a conference on the Human Environment, also known as the Stockholm Declaration, which among other things gave rise to the United Nations Environment Programme (UNEP). From this, various other projects and bodies were formed, including the IPCC in 1988 and the Intergovernmental Science-Policy Platform on Biodiversity and Ecosystem Services (IPBES) in 2012. In 1987, the World Commission on Environment and Development published the Our Common Future report, which helped establish the concept 'sustainable development' (although the UN and others had been discussing it for decades). Along with the IPCC's first report, which came out in 1990, Our Common Future helped frame the debate for the next big project: the Rio Earth Summit in 1992.

As Boutros Boutros-Ghali (1922–2016), then UN secretary-general, said at the start of the summit: 'Ultimately, if we do nothing, then the storm will break on the heads of future generations. For them it will be too late.' This sounds depressingly similar to what people are saying today, nearly three decades later.

The **United Nations Environment Programme (UNEP)** was founded in 1972 by Maurice Strong. Headquartered in Nairobi, Kenya, it has responsibility for environmental problems among UN agencies.

The **Intergovernmental Science-Policy Platform on Biodiversity and Ecosystem Services (IPBES)** was founded in 2012, and is an international body similar to the IPCC. In May 2019, it published a lengthy report on biodiversity loss.

The **Rio Earth Summit** was a major UN conference held in Rio de Janeiro, Brazil, in June 1992. Reflecting the ways in which environmental issues cross national boundaries, it hoped to provide a platform for countries to cooperate internationally on development issues.

Climategate occurred in November 2009 when a survey of the Climate Research Unit at the University of East Anglia, UK, was hacked, and thousands of emails and computer files were released online. Climate change sceptics argued it provided evidence of climate scientists manipulating data and trying to suppress critics.

The Rio Earth Summit established annual climate conferences, known as Conference of the Parties, to be held in a different country each year. There has always been a bit of a fringe to these events, with artists and protests coming along as well as formal political action. At the first, in Berlin, Germany, in 1995, most of the larger conversations were left until the Kyoto talks in 1997. Although some agreements were made in Kyoto, Japan, they did not come into force until February 2005, and by then George W. Bush (b. 1946) had already withdrawn the USA. Progress was not nearly fast enough.

The next big opportunity was the 2009 event in Copenhagen, Denmark. Climate campaigners were excited that they would finally see the sort of ambitious global action that was needed. One PR campaign even used the strapline 'Hopenhagen' (it was just after the 'Hope' branding of the Obama campaign) to shift the emphasis from 'coping' with climate change to 'hoping' for drastic action. Ultimately, their hopes were dashed. The Climategate scandal broke and the conference, after eight draft texts and all-day talks between 115 world leaders, ended with the USA and China brokering a loose accord that 'recognized' the scientific case for keeping temperature rises to no more than 2°C (3.6°F), but did not contain commitments to emissions reductions to achieve that goal. Furthermore, as discussed in Chapter 1, 2°C (3.6°F) was never safe.

A

Barack Obama (b. 1961) spun it as: 'We have come a long way but we have much further to go.' This might have sounded encouraging if, as *The New York Times* was quick to point out, it were not exactly what George H. W. Bush (1924–2018) had said at the Rio Earth Summit, 17 years earlier.

Six months later, Christiana Figueres (b. 1956), a Costa Rican diplomat, was appointed the new executive secretary of the UN Framework Convention on Climate Change. In her first few days in office, a journalist asked her if she thought a climate change agreement was possible, and she responded, 'Not in my lifetime.' But Figueres soon realized that if they were going to make action on climate change a reality, they had to rise out of the post-Copenhagen despondency and revitalize some of the optimism. Building a new climate agreement would, at least in part, be a matter of changing the tone.

In many ways, it worked. The Paris talks in 2015 did not please everyone – arguably, they were still too little, too late – but they did not crash and burn. Moreover, they helped shift attitudes towards a more 'can-do' approach, and they opened up discussion around 1.5°C (2.7°F).

The UN is not the only international player.

Indeed, one of the key shifts in the past decade has been the growth of initiatives to connect other sites of global power, beyond just the nation state. The C40 Cities Climate Leadership Group, for example, was set up in 2005 as a way of connecting mayors. There are also projects such as the RE100, which brings together influential businesses committed to 100% renewable energy. This is where some of the headlines about wind-powered beer or chocolate stem from.

A The 2015 Paris climate talks. Taking place just two weeks after major terrorist attacks, security was very tight, with strict limits on protests that usually surround such talks. After years of careful build up, the participants managed to agree a major shift to talk about keeping global warming to under 1.5°C (2.7°F) rather than 2°C (3.6°F).

B The C40 Cities Climate Leadership Group celebrates its tenth birthday in 2015 with a Clean Bus Declaration and a summit lead by the then Mayor of London, Boris Johnson. C40 Cities connects cities around the world acting on climate change. With 94 members, it represents a twelfth of the world's population.

B

These organizations have been crucial. When Donald Trump (b. 1946) threatened to pull out of Paris, a 'We're Still In' pledge speedily mobilized, with a letter signed by the mayors of Los Angeles, New York, Atlanta and more, alongside universities and major companies such as Apple, Google, Microsoft and Facebook, all stating that, whatever their president does, the 155 million Americans and $9.45 trillion of the US economy they represent still back the UN's climate process.

A   The Eiffel Tower lit up with 'No Plan B' to mark the UN Climate Change Conference coming to Paris in December 2015. These were the 21st annual UN climate talks.
B   Climate activists demonstrate in front of a Unicredit bank wearing masks inspired by the *Money Heist* series ('*La Casa de Papel*') broadcast by Netflix.
C   Extinction Rebellion protesters block traffic on the Strand, London, UK, 2019. It was part of a week-long series of protests given the code name 'Project Mushroom', a reference to how spores of the movement have spread.

We should also remember the networks of scientists on which so much environmental work relies. Some of these are run via the UN, such as the IPCC or IPBES, but they are only part of the story. There is the International Council for Science, for example. Headquartered in Paris, France, it represents other international networks of scientists, such as the International Water Association and the International Union of Soil Sciences. It is one of the world's oldest non-governmental organizations, as it can trace its history back to 1899.

A

School Strike for Climate is a international movement of young people leaving school on Fridays to protest on environmental issues. It was started by Swedish teenager Greta Thunberg who, following a summer of heat waves and wildfires, decided not to attend school until the Swedish general election in early September 2018.

Extinction Rebellion is an international movement, started in London in 2018, that uses non-violent direct action to pressure governments to act on the climate emergency.

B

C

There are also formal and informal relationships between universities, national membership groups for different disciplines – the American Geophysical Union or the British Ecological Society, for example– conferences, postgraduate programmes and journals. That we are even close to being able to tackle the environmental crises in front of us – that we can even see them at all, in some cases – is down to the early warning and detailed knowledge they provide.

There is also a wealth of activity at grassroots level. This has a long and proud tradition, and has received a recent boost from the School Strike for Climate and the Extinction Rebellion, as well as local plastic clear-up projects.

DDT is short form for dichlorodiphenyl-trichloroethane. Its insecticidal action was discovered by Swiss chemist Paul Hermann Müller for which he was awarded the Nobel Prize in Physiology or Medicine in 1948. However, following a large public outcry on its impact on bird populations, it was banned in the USA in 1972 by legislation that is credited with playing a role in saving the bald eagle from extinction.

A   John Muir, Scottish-born American naturalist, writer and founder of the Sierra Club.
B   Environmental activist David Brower, leads a protest in Arizona, USA, 1966.
C   A Greenpeace activist weeps over carcasses of harp seal pups, Canada, winter 1988.
D   A Greenpeace campaigner sprays green dye on a baby seal to make their fur worthless.

A

B

Another recent development is the fixer movement: mending workshops where local people can bring broken goods such as toasters, laptops, bicycles or clothes and work out how to fix them, with the support of skilled tradesmen. Often people come away from these workshops with their vacuum cleaner or phone still broken, because goods are not designed to be fixed, but they are still satisfied by the experience. They have learnt a lot more about how things they use every day are put together, and been inspired to use customer power to fight for better-made, fixable products. A growing political movement to see legislation in the EU to make products more repairable has arisen as a result of such activities.

Grassroots campaigns, by their very nature, often work on a local level, but this does not mean that the work stays local. They are often symbolic of larger, global issues, or reflect internationally significant moments. As global publics become more connected with each other, it is easier for localized environmental campaigning to spread and reach broader audiences.

C

D

The speed at which the School Strikes for Climate and plastic clean-up projects have sparked off each other demonstrates this.

In terms of larger, professional campaign organizations, some such as the Sierra Club (founded in 1892) are at least a century old. A number of these older ones retain a rather colonial approach. The group now known as Fauna and Flora International, for example, was founded in 1903 as the Society for the Preservation of the Wild Fauna of the Empire by a group of British naturalists and US statesmen in Africa, although it has changed a lot since then. The 1960s saw worries about biodiversity lead to the formation of the World Wildlife Fund, framed at least in part by concerns about population, with British biologist Julian Huxley (1887–1975) a key player. It also saw the foundation of the Environmental Defense Fund, whose research initially focused on the hazards of DDT, most likely prompted by the environmental classic *Silent Spring* (1962) by Rachel Carson (1907–64). The slightly more rebellious 1970s led to some new groups, actively critiquing older generations. Friends of the Earth was an explicit split from the Sierra Club, and Greenpeace was initially a campaign against nuclear bomb testing.

A

The wave of climate concern in the noughties led to the formation of some climate specific non-governmental organizations. Among these, 350.org is especially significant for its community-organizing approach, growing local hubs of social capital around divestment campaigns – especially in university campuses – which breathed new life into the movement after the disappointment of the Copenhagen talks. It has also been central in pushing a message of climate justice that emphasizes the connections between greenhouse gas emissions and other issues such as race and economic inequality.

So what can we do with these various social and political resources?

First, governments need to think, above all, about where they put their money. According to the IEA, although national fossil fuel subsidies fell in 2015, they still totalled at least $373 billion globally. Working out exactly what counts as a fossil fuel subsidy is a tricky business. Some calculate this figure to be higher and others lower, depending on how you define subsidy. But most countries subsidize fossil fuels in some way or another.

According to International Monetary Fund figures (which overall come in higher than those quoted by the IEA), the largest subsidizers in 2015 were China ($1.4 trillion), USA ($649 billion), Russia ($551 billion), EU ($289 billion) and India ($209 billion). However, when assessing these numbers, it is important to remember each country's size, the amount of goods produced in each country, and how developed their fossil fuel industry already is. All those 'made in China' labels, for example, are artefacts of another country burning through energy to make goods you use. According to the EU, within its ranks, Britain provides the most support to fossil fuels, around €12 billion a year (compared to €8.3 billion on renewable energy). In Germany, this is more than reversed, with €27 billion spent on renewable energy and €9.5 billion on fossil fuels.

It is clear we need to shift money away from fossil fuels, fast, and invest heavily in the technologies and policies that will help us live more peaceably with the rest of the planet. All the technologies described in Chapter 3 cost money, especially those that are not yet fully developed. Living with global warming is expensive too, though, either because we spend money to protect ourselves and on clean-up costs (Hurricane Katrina has been estimated at $161 billion), or because of the hit to the economy caused by the loss of cash crops such as coffee. Spending on environmental action almost always leads to economic benefits.

B

C

We also need to think more about how rich countries can shift resources to poorer ones. Countries such as the USA, Britain and France are still living off the profits of their early emissions in the Industrial Revolution, just as they are still living off the benefits of slavery. As the benefits of the Industrial Revolution were in no small part down to slavery, it is perhaps no surprise that the more radical campaigners talk about the need for climate reparations. Research published in 2019 showed that climate change was already significantly holding back the economic growth of poorer countries. Moreover, these are the countries that emit the least carbon.

This can bring up the difficult question of who is to blame for global warming. If you compare current annual emissions on a country-by-country basis, China is at the top, followed closely by the USA, then India, Russia, Japan, Germany and so on. However, if you ask which country has the highest emissions per capita, a very different pattern emerges. In this scenario, the order is USA, Australia, Canada, South Korea, Russia, Japan, Germany and only then China, one place above Britain.

A

CO$_2$ EMISSIONS PER CAPTIA (2017)
Average carbon dioxide (CO$_2$) emissions per capita measured in tonnes per year

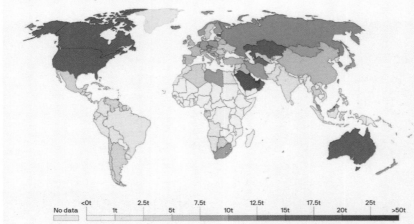

No data	<0t		2.5t		7.5t		12.5t		17.5t		25t	
		1t		5t		10t		15t		20t		>50t

Climate reparations are payments to those who are suffering from the impacts of climate change and colonialism, paid for by those descended from (and thus also inheriting the benefits of) those who caused it.

The **Wellbeing of Future Generations Act** (2016) asks public organizations to take into account the long-term effects of any decision they make.

A   Average carbon dioxide (CO_2) emissions per capita measured in tonnes per year, 2017.
B   A 'climate justice now' banner as 2,500 activists invade a coal mine in Hambach, Germany, 2017.
C   Flight attendants of the newly launched low-cost airline between South Korea and Japan, autumn 2016.

B

C

It is also worth considering cumulative emissions since the Industrial Revolution, because this offers a better sense of each country's role in causing the warming we are currently dealing with. It gives a whole new pattern again. Here, the USA is first, with China next, and the former USSR coming in third before Germany, Britain, Japan, India and France. Furthermore, it is vital to remember there is disparity within countries. Flying in Britain is a good example of this: 70% of the flights are taken by 15% of the population, with 50% of British people taking zero flights each year and around 20% saying they have never set foot on a plane.

On a more local political level, we could push governments to think beyond their standard four-year cycles – like the Wellbeing of Future Generations Act in Wales, for example – which could have clear benefits when it comes to fishing and agricultural policy, as well as carbon emissions. Similarly, there are also calls to lower the voting age to build momentum on environmental action.

A   These apples aren't just shiny; they're wrapped in plastic. As anti-plastics campaigns grow, plastic wrapping for fruit and vegetables has come under particular criticism.

B   An environmental campaigner wears a costume made of disposable plastic bags, supporting a ban on plastic bags in Los Angeles, USA, winter 2016.

C   Greenpeace activists dress as orangutans in a protest outside the offices of Nestlé in Beijing, China, 2010. The deforestation that accompanies growing palm oil for chocolate threatens the homes of endangered species such as orangutans.

D   *Gilets Jaunes* walk through tear gas during clashes with police in Paris, France, February 2019. The causes of these protests are complex, but are at least in part environmental.

We could ask our politicians to introduce bans or put up taxes on meat, flying, owning a car or plastic straws. Some campaigners want to see controls on having more than one or two kids too.

Introducing bans and tax hikes is not always the best approach though. When it comes to population control, for example, many argue that having children is a human right, or point out the long and problematic history of eugenics. For flying, you could easily end up simply pricing out poorer travellers while the rich continue to fry the planet with their aviation emissions. Palm oil perhaps offers the most interesting case study. Simply banning it would most likely displace biodiversity loss, not halt it. Palm oil, for all its problems, still produces up to nine times more oil per unit of land than alternative oil crops, such as sunflower or rapeseed.

In addition, whatever you might want to target – be it petrol, palm oil, babies or cheese – laws very rarely get tabled unless there is a very clear public interest.

Politicians also need to ensure people do not feel left out. There are two key reasons for this. The first is moral: if we believe in a just and fair society, we should ensure we do not leave this stance behind as we take radical action to tackle environmental crises. The other is practical: if people feel left out, they will slow our ability to act.

There are plenty of people with power who would very much like to keep the status quo, and such people will pick up any sense of disaffection with environmental action and amplify it. The *Gilets Jaunes* movement is becoming the cautionary tale de jour for environmental activists. The causes of this are complex, but it has been at least partly influenced by rising fuel prices, which some have painted as environmental policies that disproportionately hit the already squeezed bank balances of the working and lower middle classes.

Gilets Jaunes, also known as the yellow vests movement, is a populist political movement with members spanning a range of the political spectrum, emphasizing issues of economic justice. It began in France in November 2018.

C

D

A **Green New Deal**
proposes a stimulus
programme that
aims to address
climate change and
economic inequality
together, with a nod to
Franklin D. Roosevelt's
economic reforms
in response to the
Great Depression. The
phrase a 'Green New
Deal' has been used
on and off for decades,
but it has been given a
particular boost since
the 2018 US midterm
elections when the
Sunrise Movement
started actively
campaigning for it with
Democrat politicians.

A Democrat Congresswoman
Alexandria Ocasio-Cortez
announces new Green
New Deal legislation, 2019.
B The Instagram account
@Aningslösainfluencers
('clueless influencers' in
Swedish) draws attention
to social media influencers'
air travel and the impact
they have on the environment.

There is a growing body of social science research showing that if people have a stake in environmental action they are more likely support it.

This is one of the reasons why the US Sunrise Movement's call for a Green New Deal and Extinction Rebellion's call for citizens' juries on climate change (inspired by a model that helped changed abortion law in Ireland) have the power they do: they put a vital focus on public participation and a just transition.

A

Uruguay, Shanghai, New York och Paris på **fyra månader**

linneklund

10,6 ton CO2

Eller 26 års-flygbudgetar

linneklund Speedy Gonzales crew off to Paris

#speedygonzales

@matildadjerf

London - Kapstaden - **Manchester hittills i år!**

5,2 ton CO2 och 13 personers flygbudgetar borta

@matildadjerf

#SOLIDARITET

Malaysia

michellesvendsen

3,6 ton CO2

Planeten mår

michellesvendsen Jag mår.

As an individual reading this book, where can you start?

One popular option is to give up meat and dairy, because a plant-based diet makes far less of an ecological impact than a meat-based one. The carbon footprint of a vegan diet is about 60% lighter than a meat and dairy one. Others will tell you to quit flying. In Sweden, Greta Thunberg's straightforward refusal to fly inspired a whole new word, *flygskam*, or flight shame. You might also find scientists telling you to simply talk about environmental issues more. At the same time, there are those who argue that anything you do on an individual level is pointless and that we need to fight for dramatic structural change. There is truth in all of these ideas, but they are also, in a way, all selling magic beans. When it comes to climate change, we do not need 'one thing'. We need to act in a whole range of areas – from what we eat to how we get around – at all levels of society.

A

If we want powerful environmental action, then we need to be savvy political operators, and that includes paying attention not only to policy makers and big business, but also to culture and society at large.

Arguably, there is no such thing as an individual when it comes to our modern environmental crisis. It is undoubtedly true that we have built an Anthropocene that is incredibly unequal. Some people reap the benefits of our exploitation of nature far more than others. Similarly, some are left far more at risk by environmental damage. But we are all connected in this.

B

The idea of a personal carbon footprint, for example, can be a useful heuristic for looking at the impact of some of our personal choices, but nothing we do that expends any meaningful amount of carbon is done alone. We are only able to emit so much carbon because we are social animals. We might buy a plane ticket to travel alone, but we are sitting on the aircraft with other passengers and a whole global industrial infrastructure around us. Even if you piloted a plane, on your own, you would be drawing on the skills of generations of aviation engineers, as well as the chains of people who built the plane, mined the materials and so on. To unravel our carbon addiction, we have to work with others.

Many psychologists of environmental behaviour argue that lifestyle change can build momentum for greater change. We humans are social; we need social cues before we do most things. People do not spring into action just because they see smoke; they spring into action because they see others rushing in with water. The same principle applies to taking action on environmental crisis.

A

People are more likely to cut down on meat or flying, buy solar panels or start using a reusable coffee cup, for example, when they see other people doing the same. Moreover, when this individual action starts to become a cultural shift, politicians and people in other key areas of power (such as the mainstream media or large businesses) start to act, which in turn provides even stronger social cues, until wanting to take action becomes normal.

It can be daunting to work out where to start. Should you go vegan, join a protest, give up flying, go plastic free? One answer is to pick something you can enjoy. You will be more successful and you will be more infectious, too. If you choose to try a plant-based diet, do not just go vegan for a month, involve your friends and family, too. Cook up a plant-based feast to show off all the great new recipes you have found.

Share recipes for low carbon food with your friends. If you have a work canteen, see if you can initiate some meat-free days, or ask local cafes and restaurants to introduce them. Write to your favourite brands about what they are doing to tackle climate change, and ask your politicians how they are going to ensure our agricultural policies are up to the environmental challenge. Let change spread. The Swedish *flygskam* has not only led to a drop in flights in that country, it has prompted *lentohapea* in Finland, *vliegschaamte* in the Netherlands and *flugscham* in Germany.

The same pattern works whichever way you take action. Think about what you want to do yourself, then think about how you can involve other people. Tell politicians what you have done and pester them to create policies that will help all of us up our ambition. Most importantly, scale up your action.

A   A public water fountain in London, UK, part of a network installed following public outcry over public waste and an agreement between the mayor and the local water company.

B   An animal rights activist holds a placard with 'Meat melts the world. Harden your Resolve. Go Vegan.' Vegan activists have, in places, been accused of hijacking the larger and more complex issue of climate action.

C   A police officer in London, UK, walks past public telephone boxes daubed with the words 'vegan' and 'rebel'. The number of vegans in Great Britain quadrupled between 2014 and 2018, although vegans remain fewer than 1.5% of the population.

Positive spillover is a psychological term for changes in behaviour, when one positive shift leads to another. For example, you start exercising, making you think of yourself as a healthier person, leading you in turn to drop a range of unhealthy habits.

As psychologists of environmental behaviour will point out, for all that there can be positive spillover effects, there can also be negative ones, in which you complete a vegan January challenge and book a trans-Atlantic return flight to celebrate.

A   The then 15-year-old Greta Thunberg starts her school strike for the climate in August 2018, sitting alone outside the Swedish parliament building.
B   Just over a year since Thurnberg's first lone strike, she addresses a crowd during the New York City Climate Strike rally. Organizers estimate that globally 7.6 million people took part in the strike, in 185 countries.

We are in a crisis situation, and small discrete steps will not suffice.

A

Whatever you decide to do, spread the word. One of the biggest problems we have when it comes to tackling climate change and biodiversity is simply that we avoid discussing the problems. It is understandable; maybe we find it uncomfortable to talk about land degradation at the dinner table. But by talking about these issues we can normalize the need to take radical action, and keep the pressure on politicians and other people in power. It is also how we will learn to deal emotionally with the damage we have already done and to debate the decisions ahead.

B

Conclusion

A

This book opened with some questions. What, in the 2020s, does it mean to save the planet? Can we? Should we? Whose planet is it anyway?

A traditional green answer is that the planet is so much more than us, and that we can and indeed must 'save' it, or at least fight those who threaten the other species who share the Earth with us. To do so, we probably need to be more humble in the face of nature, to step back and give it more space.

Anthropocene thinking challenges this. Or at least invites us to a vision of the Earth dominated by humans. We might draw back in revulsion at this, to aim to end the age of the human with some sort of managed retreat. Alternatively, we could run with it, follow the logic that we can shape the world so why not build more to bend it to our aims? Let's hack our planet, with geoengineering projects, massive rewilding, CRISPR trees, whatever works.

There is also a middle ground, one that makes peace with humans' use of technology while also ensuring space for the rest of nature to thrive. We can blend nature-based solutions such as rewilding and tree planting with more political and technological options, from giving indigenous people power over land to technology-based innovations such as plyscrapers, solar and wind power (big and small), CRISPR-boosted crops and microbes that munch through plastics, assuming we are comfortable they are safe.

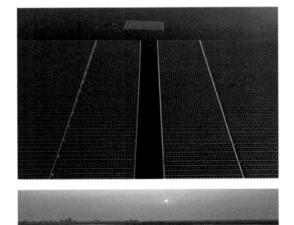

A Starlings gather in a murmuration over an electricity pylon in the south of Scotland.
B This floating solar farm in Anhui province (China's coal centre) has been developed on a lake caused by a coal mine that collapsed and flooded over a decade ago due to over-mining. When completed, the solar farm's 166,000 panels should produce enough electricity to power a city, making it one of the largest floating solar projects in the world.

B

A   A stork caught in plastic packaging. Images of wildlife tangled in plastic grab media attention, but we also need to worry about plastics pollution we cannot see. Microplastics have been found in tap water and rain around the world.

B   Villages in southern Bangladesh, water locked due to flooding, summer 2019. Bangladesh is one the countries most vulnerable to the impacts of climate change. Researchers warn that Bangladesh could lose more than 10% of its land to rising seas in the next few decades, displacing 18 million people.

A

Possibly the most profound thing we can take from Anthropocene thinking is that we have to live with a planet we have damaged. Saving the Earth in the 2020s – or perhaps the sorts of activities we used to call saving the Earth – is about accepting, grieving for and adapting to the destruction humans have caused. We are inheriting a mess. In the 1980s and 1990s, when people started campaigning about climate change in earnest, people would talk about solving global warming. Roll on a few decades of inaction, and now we have to cope with a major dose of climate change and biodiversity loss while also still battling to prevent more. It is less about solving the problem and more about managing it.

Humans may have made the Anthropocene epoch, but can they survive it?

B

We can hope. As a *Nature* paper argued in 2017, it is not geophysically impossible for us to keep to 1.5°C (2.7°F) degrees global warming. That was in 2017 though. Moreover, there is a long, winding road between something being not geophysically impossible, and it being a social, economic, political and cultural reality. Plus, 1.5°C (2.7°F) is not exactly ideal. We are already living with the impacts of around 1°C (1.8°F), and for some people, it is already hurting.

The planet might not be 'saved' in a traditional sense, but it can be habitable. The space we have left for action is diminishing even faster than the ice caps, but we still have that space. The time to act is now. Environmental activists have been saying this for decades, but that does not make it any less true, just more urgent.

There is an oft-repeated Obama line that we are the first generation to really feel the impacts of climate change, and the last generation with the power to do anything about it. It is more complex than 'we have ten years to save the world or we go extinct', but the 2020s are crucial in terms of changing how we live. The window of opportunity is getting smaller every day, but it exists.

A People dressed in white crowd the Olympic park to form a glacier during the 'Global Climate March'. Organized by environmental NGOs on 29 November 2015 in Munich, southern Germany, the march took place on the eve of the official opening of a 195-nation UN climate summit in Paris.

B A solar installer in the south of England puts the finishing touches to a pilot study to power trains directly with renewable energy. The project, which was first conceived by community groups looking to build locally owned solar farms in response to controversies over fracking, could help accelerate the decarbonization of railways around the world.

C The crew of a two-year NASA project investigating the changing conditions of the Arctic retrieves a canister of supplies from sea ice melt ponds.

c

Are we drifting into a position where we take light, half-hearted environmental action, all a bit too late? Where we keep the worst storms at bay, but it is still bad; the billionaires are able to insulate themselves in solar-powered pods, with the rest left to drown, starve and burn? Possibly, but we still have the option to avoid this fate. Moreover, we have a variety of choices regarding how we might go about building the sort of planet on which we can thrive.

Instead of debating whether we should act or not, we should be battling over how we go about it.

A

If we make the type of profound, radical changes we need, we will be building a whole new world. What do we want this world to look like? What political ideologies do we want to govern it? Who do we want to be its architects? Silicon Valley, the fixer movement, the climate strikers? What new cultures do we want? Less state control, or more? Less consumerism, or different consumerism? We still have choices, and it is vital that we discuss the available options; decide what we want and what compromises we're willing to make with others who might think differently.

Change is coming, either way. It might come from society, a shift in the way we choose to live our lives, or it might come from the sky, in the form of storms, or the soil, as it gradually blows away. It is up to us to decide what sort of change we want to live with.

A   Kolmanskop, Namibia,
     once boosted a ballroom,
     a casino, a hospital with
     the first 2-ray station in
     the southern hemisphere
     and Africa's first tram.
     Today, it's a ghost town.
B   The futuristic redesign
     for a highway in Bao'an,
     China. Instead of simply
     enlarging the road,
     the designers propose
     a smaller, more fluid
     route built for a range
     of transport types.

It might be a myth to say that 'we are all in this together', because some people are hurting more than others just as some are polluting more than others. But we are all in this whether we like it or not. You personally can have a powerful role; just work out how to invite others to come with you. Be the person who takes action and gets other people to join in, whether you do that by shifting what you eat or how you travel, or by supergluing yourself to a railing on the street.

We are the generation that gets to save humanity. You might not want to be cast in that role, but that is where we are now.

At least we still have the chance to save the planet. Future humans might not be able to say the same.

B

Further Reading

Digital

Carbon Brief,
www.carbonbrief.org

Climate Change News,
www.climatechangenews.com

Drawdown, www.drawdown.org

Earther,
www.earther.gizmodo.com

Ed Hawkins's blog, www.
climate-lab-book.ac.uk/
author/ehawkins

Flash Forward podcast,
www.flashforwardpod.com

ICUN Issues Briefs, www.iucn.
org/resources/issues-briefs

Kate Marvel's blog, www.
scientificamerican.com/
author/kate-marvel

Katharine Hayhoe's Twitter lists,
www.twitter.com/KHayhoe/
lists/scientists-who-do-
climate and www.twitter.com/
KHayhoe/lists/experts-who-
talk-climate

NASA Vital Signs Project, www.
climate.nasa.gov/vital-signs

Sci Dev Net, www.scidev.net/
global

Tamsin Edwards's PLOS blog,
www.blogs.plos.org/models

WWF's Footprint Calculator,
www.footprint.wwf.org.uk

Print

**Berners-Lee, Mike and Clark,
Duncan,** *The Burning Question:
We Can't Burn Half the World's
Oil, Coal and Gas. So How
Do We Quit?* (London: Profile;
Vancouver: Greystone
Books, 2013)

Berners-Lee, Mike, *How Bad
Are Bananas: The Carbon
Footprint of Everything*
(London: Profile, 2010)

Carson, Rachel, *The Sea
Around Us* (New York,
NY: Oxford University
Press, 1951)

Carson, Rachel, *Silent Spring*
(Boston, MA: Houghton
Mifflin Company, 1962)

Emmott, Stephen, *Ten Billion*
(New York, NY: Vintage;
London: Penguin, 2013)

Flannery, Tim, *We Are the
Weather Makers: The Story
of Global Warming* (London:
Penguin, 2007)

Freese, Barbara, *Coal: A Human
History* (Reading, MA: Perseus,
2003)

Gardiner, Beth, *Choked: The
Age of Air Pollution and the
Fight for a Cleaner Future*
(London: Granta, 2019)

Goulson, Dave, *A Sting in the
Tale* (London: Jonathan Cape,
2013)

Hansen, James, *Storms of My
Grandchildren: The Truth About
the Coming Climate Catastrophe
and Our Last Chance to Save
Humanity* (London; New York,
NY: Bloomsbury, 2009)

Haraway, Donna, *The
Companion Species Manifesto:
Dogs, People, and Significant
Otherness* (Chicago, IL:
Prickly Paradigm Press, 2003)

Haraway, Donna, *Simians,
Cyborgs and Women:
The Reinvention of Nature*
(New York, NY: Routledge,
1991)

Jackson, Roland, *The Ascent of John Tyndall* (Oxford: Oxford University Press, 2018)

Klein, Naomi, *This Changes Everything: Capitalism vs. the Climate* (New York, NY: Simon & Schuster, 2015)

Kolbert, Elizabeth, *Field Notes from a Catastrophe: Man, Nature, and Climate Change* (London: Bloomsbury, 2006)

Kolbert, Elizabeth, *The Sixth Extinction: An Unnatural History* (New York, NY: Henry Holt and Company, 2014)

Latour, Bruno, *Facing Gaia: Eight Lectures on the New Climatic Regime,* trans. Catherine Porter (Cambridge; Medford, MA: Polity, 2017)

Lynas, Mark, *Six Degrees: Our Future on a Hotter Planet* (London: Fourth Estate, 2007)

Madrigal, Alexis, *Powering the Dream: The History and Promise of Green Technology* (Cambridge, MA: Da Capo Press, 2011)

Maslin, Mark, *Climate Change: A Very Short Introduction* (Oxford; New York, NY: Oxford University Press, 2009)

Maslin, Mark and Lewis, Simon L., *The Human Planet: How We Created the Anthropocene* (London: Pelican; New Haven, CT: Yale University Press, 2018)

Morton, Oliver, *Eating the Sun: The Everyday Miracle of How Plants Power the Planet* (London: Harper Perennial, 2009)

Morton, Oliver, *The Planet Remade: How Geoengineering Could Change the World* (Princeton, NJ: Princeton University Press, 2015)

Morton, Tim, *Being Ecological* (London: Pelican; Cambridge, MA: MIT Press, 2018)

Nicolson, Marjorie Hope, *Mountain Gloom and Mountain Glory: The Development of the Aesthetics of the Infinite* (Ithaca, NY: University of Cornell Press, 1959)

Nye, David E., *American Techno-logical Sublime* (Cambridge, MA: MIT Press, 1994)

Oreskes, Naomi and Conway, Erik M., *Merchants of Doubt: How a Handful of Scientists Obscured the Truth on Issues from Tobacco Smoke to Global Warming* (New York, NY: Bloomsbury, 2011)

Rhodes, Richard, *Energy: A Human History* (New York, NY: Simon & Schuster, 2019)

Rich, Nathaniel, *Losing Earth: A Recent History* (New York, NY: MCD, 2019)

Smedley, Tim, *Clearing the Air: The Beginning and the End of Air Pollution* (London: Bloomsbury Sigma, 2019)

Thunberg, Greta, *No One Is Too Small to Make a Difference* (London: Penguin, 2019)

Vince, Gaia, *Adventures in the Anthropocene: A Journey to the Heart of the Planet We Made* (Minneapolis, MN: Milkweed Editions, 2014)

Weart, Spencer R., *The Discovery of Global Warming* (Cambridge, MA: Harvard University Press, 2003)

Picture Credits

Every effort has been made to locate and credit copyright holders of the material reproduced in this book. The author and publisher apologize for any omissions or errors, which can be corrected in future editions.

a = above, b = below,
c = centre, l = left, r = right

69 Dea/Biblioteca Ambrosiana/Getty Images

70–1 © Alex Webb/ Magnum Photos

72 © Jonas Bendiksen/ Magnum Photos

73 Timothy Fadek/Corbis via Getty Images

74a Stefano Montesi/ Corbis via Getty Images

74b Drew Angerer/ Getty Images

75l Andia/Universal Images Group via Getty Images

75r Chuck Eckert/Alamy Stock Photo

76al Ulrich Baumgarten via Getty Images

76ar Arterra/Universal Images Group via Getty Images

76bl blickwinkel/Alamy Stock Photo

76br Paul Mcerlane/ Bloomberg via Getty Images

78a Helmut Meyer Zur Capellen/imageBROKER/ Shutterstock

78b VCG/VCG via Getty Images

79 Yang Huafeng/China News Service/VCG via Getty Images

80 Courtesy Better Burger

81 Reuters/Mike Segar

82 The University of Queensland, Brisbane

83 Courtesy designer Yulia Kigel, H.I.T - Holon Institute of Technology, Israel, (Tutor Shimon (Jogol) Sandhaus)

84 Climeworks

85a Melanie Stetson Freeman/The Christian Science Monitor via Getty Images

85b Canadian Press/ Shutterstock

86a Reuters/Paulo Santos

86b Halldor Kolbeins/AFP/ Getty Images

87 Ozkan Bilgin/Anadolu Agency/Getty Images

88 Nadezda Murmakova

89 Van Vuuren, D. et al. (2018) 'Alternative pathways to the 1.5C target reduce the need for negative emission technologies', *Nature Climate Change*, doi:10.1038/s41558-018-0119-8

90 David Liittschwager/ National Geographic Creative

91 NASA

92l Matthias Schrader/ AP/Shutterstock

92r Science Photo Library/ Alamy Stock Photo

93l NASA

93r John MacNeill

94 Zoonar GmbH/ Alamy Stock Photo

95 Reuters/Sukree Sukplang

96 Turenscape

97 Jasper Juinen/ Bloomberg via Getty Images

98 Jerónimo Alba/ Alamy Stock Photo

99 Orjan Ellingvag/ Alamy Stock Photo

100–1 Richard Robinson

102 Artyom Geodakyan/ TASS via Getty Images

103 Sony Ramany/NurPhoto via Getty Images

104 Sipa/Shutterstock

106 Christophe Morin/ Bloomberg via Getty Images

107 Velar Grant/ZUMA Wire/ ZUMAPRESS.com/ Alamy Live News

108 Patrick Kovarik/ AFP/Getty Images

109a Nicolò Campo/ LightRocket via Getty Images

109b John Keeble/ Getty Images

110a Photo12/Universal Images Group via Getty Images

110b Arthur Schatz/The LIFE Picture Collection via Getty Images

111 Tom Stoddart Archive/ Getty Images

112 Qilai Shen/Bloomberg via Getty Images

113l Andrew Burton/ Getty Images

113r Creative Touch Imaging Ltd./NurPhoto via Getty Images

114 Our World In Data

115a Markus Heine/SOPA Images/LightRocket via Getty Images

115b Yonhap/EPA/ Shutterstock

116a Paula Bronstein/ Getty Images

116b Patrick T. Fallon/ Bloomberg via Getty Images

117l WENN Rights Ltd/ Alamy Stock Photo

117r Michel Stoupak/ NurPhoto via Getty Images

118 Al Drago/Bloomberg via Getty Images

119 Aningslösa influencers / Instagram

120 Luke Sharrett/ Bloomberg via Getty Images

121 Michele Tantussi/ Bloomberg via Getty Images

122 Photo by Leon Neal/ Getty Images

123a Jay Directo/AFP/ Getty Images

123b Tolga Akmen/AFP/ Getty Images

124 Michael Campanella/ Getty Images

125 Ron Adar/SOPA Images/ LightRocket via Getty Images

126–7 Christopher Furlong/ Getty Images

128 Jeff J. Mitchell/ Getty Images

129 Kevin Frayer/ Getty Images

130 © John Cancalosi/ naturepl.com

131 Mohammad Saiful Islam/ NurPhoto via Getty Images

132a Sven Hoppe/AFP/ Getty Images

132b Andrew Aitchison/ In Pictures via Getty Images

133 NASA/Kathryn Hansen

134 Hoberman/Universal Images Group via Getty Images

135 Avoid Obvious Architects (USA) + TETRA Architects & Planners (Hong Kong)

Index

References to illustrations are in **bold**.

Acknowledgments:
Thanks to my teammates at the climate charity Possible, especially Esther Griffin and Max Wakefield. Royalties from this book will go to support our work raising ambition on climate action. Thanks also to everyone I worked with at UCL, Imperial College, SPRU, City University, Storythings, the Road to Paris and the Science Museum – I've learnt so much from you all. Finally, thanks also to Jane Laing, Phoebe Lindsley, Isabel Jessop and Tristan de Lancey at Thames & Hudson, Matthew Taylor for his clear critiques, and to Mairi Ryan at the RSA for making the introduction.

MIX
Paper from responsible sources
FSC® C112556
FSC
www.fsc.org

First published in 2020 in the United States of America by Thames & Hudson Inc., 500 Fifth Avenue, New York, New York 10110

www.thamesandhudsonusa.com

Library of Congress Control Number: 2019940746

ISBN 978-0-500-29530-4

Printed and bound in in Slovenia by DZS-Grafik d.o.o.